The

Harvesters

The Story of the Migrant People

LOUISA R. SHOTWELL

The

Harvesters

The Story of the Migrant People

Doubleday & Company, Inc.

Garden City, New York

1961

Library of Congress Catalog Card Number 61–9552

Copyright © 1961 by Louisa R. Shotwell
All Rights Reserved
Printed in the United States of America

First Edition

Contents

Foreword

The many words that have been written about migrant workers add up to a mountain of paper: magazine and newspaper features, novels, doctoral dissertations, sections of sociological texts, studies and recommendations, legislative hearings. Yet exploration has not turned up any book that unfolds the present panorama for the general reader—whose daily diet, if there were no migrants, would be conspicuously low in vegetables and fruits.

It has been the intent in *The Harvesters* to portray the complex setting in which migrant families of different ethnic backgrounds live and work; to identify the thorny issues their migrancy raises for themselves, for the communities and the states that recruit their labor, and for the national economy; and to attempt a foreshadowing of what lies ahead for them.

The Fontanezes, the Gradys, the Vinsons, the Yazzies, Felipe Ovieto, Armando and Rosa Santiago—all of these are fictitious; so are the growers and the crew leaders whom they encounter. But their situation is authentic, and so are their experiences. Everything that happens to them has happened to real migrant people somewhere.

Many persons have contributed to the making of this book. The idea for it stemmed from a pamphlet I wrote three years ago at the request of the national migrant committee of the National Council of Churches (*This is the Migrant,* Friendship Press); the basic material appears there in capsule form. Government personnel, several growers, and uncounted numbers of migrant people have been generous with time, information, and guidance. Special appreciation goes to Edith Lowry, national director of the Migrant Ministry, for her constant encouragement and her patient combing of much of the manuscript in the interests of accuracy.

Louisa R. Shotwell

Brooklyn Heights
February 22, 1961

The Citizen Worker

1. CARVED WALNUT IN A HEN HOUSE:

The Fontanez Family

The Spanish American workers in industrial agriculture are largely landless people, newcomers or second generation, marginal people with little status, few possessions, and a fair amount of personal and social disorganization.
—*Lyle Saunders, in a speech called "The Spanish-speaking People in Cultural Transition."*

In sunshine freighted with the humid sweetness that can dog a Missouri May, a squatting Pablo rocked back on his heels, braced the palms of his hands in the ground behind him, and pondered the curious ways of a man's mood. To be precise, his own mood.

Two strawberry rows away knelt his wife Annunciata, her picking rhythm slower than Pablo's but unbroken by introspection and good for eight quarts an hour at nine cents a quart; in the rows beyond her, his son Juan, his daughter Elena, his son Pedro; to his right and off by herself (he did not turn his head to look but he knew she was there) Dolores his daughter-in-law, Juan's wife, soon to make him the second time a grandfather.

His family surrounded him, as they should. After three

days of idling rain the weather gave bright promise. The berries grew firm to the touch and lush for piece-rate picking. Why, then, was he not exuberant?

Partly he knew and partly he did not know. What gave the weight to his spirit was the part he did not know. (When you understand a trouble, you may see it as the will of God and you live with it; you do not kick against the pricks. What you do not know, this it is that shadows.)

Caramba! Such absurdity! He, Pablo, forty-one years old, prince among strawberry pickers, father of four living and three dead, and a grandfather, to suffer this heaviness of heart simply and exactly because he could not account to himself for the taciturnity of his father and mother. Yet there it was. Scarcely since he was a child in the mountains of Mexico could he remember seeing Manuel (his father) so stern or Felicia (his mother) with such a tightness of the lips.

The old one, his father Manuel, sitting stiff on the edge of the bed (a bed carved head and foot with oak leaves and acorns, a walnut monster set square in the center of Mr. Van Leyden's onetime hen house, now for the duration of the picking season the sleeping-cooking-eating-washing-living place of ten Fontanezes), speaking in Spanish (for truly he knew no English though it was eighteen years since he crossed the border at Eagle Pass), dipping his *tortilla* in his morning coffee as Juan had learned in the Navy to do with a doughnut, said:

"No. Felicia and I, today we do not go to the fields. We have business to care for."

Business!

When Pablo asked, as making a joke, "Business here, *mío padre*, eight hundred miles from Crescent City, Texas?" Manuel did not smile, did not explain, did not indeed say one more word. It was Felicia who spoke then, and she said only:

"Ramona stays here with us. This sun is hotter than Crescent City. It is better she keep Miguel in from the strawberries."

(Ramona, the long black braids, the ready smile, the ten-year-old little mother to Dolores' and Juan's Miguel, saying always, "I pretend he's mine.")

Perhaps Annunciata spoke truly ten days ago in Crescent City. Perhaps, as she then said, it was wrong to carry the old ones with them in the truck to Missouri for the strawberries, on to Illinois asparagus, to Ohio tomatoes, to Arkansas cotton, to God knows where before the October cotton in the Texas Panhandle and back to Crescent City hardly in time for the Christmas fiesta.

It was not that she argued about it. Annunciata never argued, never nagged; she only murmured. And when Pablo issued a firm and dignified "No," the murmur stopped.

But to Manuel, Pablo had never learned to say a "No" of any kind.

In Crescent City, two days before they were to leave, his father announced:

"We go with you on the strawberries, Felicia and I." And that was that. As Annunciata did not dispute Pablo, so he, Pablo, did not dispute Manuel.

Was this, then, the real trouble, that at forty-one he was not yet the head of the family? Yet this was not a new thing, and knowing this, he had long accepted it. If only, that is, he understood why the father Manuel remained so somber, so adamant, saying just no, they would not go to the strawberries today, they had business.

Assuredly it was not sensible.

True, the three days of rain had made the living for ten in the hen house rather dense. It was better with a clear sky when the walnut monster could be rolled outdoors at sunrise to give room inside for moving around, washing, shaving, dressing, cooking, eating. Yet they would fare worse before they saw Crescent City again, that he knew.

It was very good when they drove the truck into Mr. Van

Leyden's yard three days ago, the tenth of May, exactly to the day as they promised a year ago to return. Mr. Van Leyden, the strawberry grower, stood under the horse-chestnut tree. He saw them. He waved. He shouted. He rushed over and he shook hands all around and he called his wife to come out and the three young Van Leydens too.

"Mother, come, bring the children. The Fontanezes are here."

That is what he said, and this is what he did. He went with them himself to the hen house to show what he had done to make it better for their comfort than last year: a different oil-stove, three burners with clean wicks; a screen at the door to keep out the mosquitoes; and for Miguel, a clothesbasket crib. What matter if Miguel had grown so tall since a year ago that the clothesbasket did not fit him so well? Surely Manuel must appreciate what a friendship Mr. Van Leyden and Pablo had together.

Ah well, time walks; meditation picks no strawberries. Perhaps tonight Manuel will tell of his great business. Business indeed.

Truly that evening when they came back from the fields there was a change, and this Pablo did not need to hear in words; he saw. Right there, twenty feet from the hen house, grew a new structure, a *casita* not five feet high, square, flat-topped, roofed with wood and faced on the sides with chicken wire. Beside it stood Manuel, stern no longer, relaxed, beaming, a proprietary hand resting on the roof of this dollhouse. In its doorway sat Felicia, black skirts spread out before her on the ground and tiny bare brown feet peeking out at the end of them, head proud like a bird and black *rebozo* just grazing the lintel.

Díos gracias, the taciturnity had fled. Manuel had his audience; this was his moment.

"Three days ago I see it when we drive into the yard, exactly there where Señor Van Leyden stands under the horse-chestnut tree. I see it, but then I do not know what I see. Last night I remember and it come to me what I see and what I must do. Today I take Ramona with me—to speak the English, of course, with Mr. Van Leyden. Say to him, I tell her, that little house under the horse-chestnut tree, Felicia and I, we want to buy it. We will move it over beside the hen house to live in for the picking time. We will work it out in strawberries.

"Señor Van Leyden tells her, say to him take it and welcome. It is nothing. It is an old squirrel cage, but the squirrels have died and the children do not care to have others. But ask him, Ramona, why does Manuel want it, he said. It is so small. It will not do to live in. Manuel Fontanez cannot stand upright in it. And I say to Ramona, ask him, Ramona, I say, does *he* sleep standing upright? Say to him maybe that is the way a Dutch strawberry grower sleep but not Manuel, the Texas picker. Say to him that inside here, Felicia and I, we can find the privacy. That is what we yearn to have.

"Pablo, my son, *this* was our business. It is cared for. Tonight we sleep in the privacy, Felicia and I. Tomorrow? Tomorrow we go with you on the strawberries, Manuel, Felicia, Ramona, Miguel, everybody!"

2. WILL THE
PICKERS COME?

The migrant worker's year is a string of beads—
a week of employment here, another there, un-
certainly tied together with travel in search of
work.

—*Farm Labor Fact Book.*

Every spring the Fontanez family and other thousands fan
out from the Southwest in search of work in crops.

A minority of them migrate entirely inside the state they call
home. There are a few states where, during every month of the
year, one crop or another demands hand labor. A California
migrant cycle may go from winter cotton to Imperial Valley
vegetables, then on to San Joaquin apricots to peaches to beans
to tomatoes to Fresno grapes, and meet itself again in fall and
winter cotton. Within Texas, cotton picking begins in July in
the Rio Grande Valley and moves up the coast to central Texas;
the harvest comes to a climax in the Panhandle in October and
then dwindles through west Texas to a December end; meantime in the lower Rio Grande Valley and that fabulous sector
that calls itself the Winter Garden there is vegetable and citrus
harvest in winter and on through spring and early summer.

But most Spanish American migrants cross a score or more of

state lines in the course of a crop season. Some start out from New Mexico or Arizona or California or Colorado. Those from Texas, where the greatest number have some kind of home base, are found during a single year working in thirty-two states.

Such are the hazards of weather, blight, market slumps, labor surplus, and time eaten up in travel and job hunting that if there exists a migrant who has found work for any fifty-two consecutive weeks, either within a single state or across the country, nobody has tracked him down.

Migrants may or may not return to home base for the winter. One Texas Mexican family turned up in the central New York State bean harvest four years after leaving the Texas community they still speak of as home. For some, home base is a house of their own somewhere across the tracks in the Mexican quarter of a southwestern town. Manuel Fontanez' wooden unpainted three rooms in the *colonia* of Crescent City was built by the family themselves on a thirty-foot-square plot. To get the land they paid ten dollars down and a dollar a month whenever the man came around to collect. (Finally he stopped coming, and in time they heard he had moved to California.)

The house has in each room one glass window and one naked electric light bulb; it has an old-fashioned icebox only rarely containing ice but convenient for storing staples, an outdoor water faucet shared by half a dozen neighbors, a porch with two front doors, and a market value of eight hundred dollars. It does not trouble the Fontanezes that they have no deed to the property. They know it is theirs, and it does not occur to them that their possession of it may be threatened.

Some families consider their home a cabin in a distant migrant labor camp, the door padlocked against their return. For others the symbol of home is no more than the mental image of a camp where they have been before and to which they hope sometime to go back, with no padlock and no cabin designated in their own minds or anybody else's as theirs; everything they own in the world journeys with them as they follow the crops by truck or jalopy. Still others make no pretense at having a home base of any kind.

Some follow a familiar pattern from season to season, returning year after year to the same growers. Some, like the Fontanezes, travel in small immediate family groups; others move with families expanded by relatives of relatives to forty or fifty or seventy-five. Still others may be members of very much larger crews impersonally assembled afresh every season by labor contractors. More likely than not these never know by name or face the owner of the crop they are working in; they work not for Mr. Johnson or Mr. Brown or Mr. Van Leyden; they work in cherries or cotton or on the beans. Indeed, the odds are increasingly good that the owner is not a man at all but a corporation. Many Spanish Americans prefer the smaller groups. They set great store by their personal relationship with the farmer; the opportunity to identify themselves with his interests attracts them more than does work in a large-scale operation in which they feel no real sense of participation.

Unknown numbers set forth without a known destination, depending on roadside signs of "Tomato Pickers Wanted" or on newspaper displays asking for peach thinners or radio voices pleading for almond knockers. Or they count on that mystical instrument, the migrant grapevine, to tell them where sugar beets or broccoli or potatoes or carrots or lettuce may need extra hands for hoeing or thinning or harvesting.

The more knowledgeable among the family heads make contact with Farm Placement offices, affiliates of the United States Employment Service maintained in an attempt to perform the staggering role of mustering enough and not too many workers in the right place at the right time. Others shun these offices because Farm Placement personnel seem to smack of government authority and because they ask questions: in Latin-American minds questions from anybody in authority too often symbolize a prelude to jail. The Fontanezes share this fear of authority; they keep a healthy distance from employment offices. As a result, they have more than once had the disquieting experience of hearing that three hundred workers are needed in a particular crop, only to arrive there in company with droves of others like them to find that the three hundred jobs have been filled by workers recruited through employment service channels. Yet it takes more than half a dozen such incidents to dissipate their dread of formal face-to-face dealings with officials.

The eight-hundred-mile leg of the Fontanez journey to Missouri is a short one compared to some. The initial trek may carry them all the way to Idaho for potatoes, or to Wisconsin for asparagus or cherries, or to Michigan for sugar beets or blueberries. A good number of Texas Mexicans head first for Oregon, where laborers of Spanish American ancestry are welcomed for the early sugar beet and onion work because they are "accustomed to stoop labor and have for years engaged in this work." South Dakota acknowledges its indebtedness to them for the arduous weeding and thinning of 5300 acres of sugar beets, a harvest need that in this state lasts from mid-May to mid-July.

Some of the Latin crews (they prefer this euphemism, for they have learned from experience the opprobrium that attaches to the word "Mexican") make straight for the state of Washington, a northwest journey from south Texas upward of twenty-four hundred miles, where seasonal harvest needs extend from April to October and reach their peak in June. For this trip the customary departure time is three in the morning, allowing a day and a night to Las Cruces, New Mexico, another day and night across Arizona to Blythe, California, and a third twenty-four-hour lap to carry them into Washington. A few hours of rest are usually taken at noon, some sleeping in the truck and some on the ground by the side of the road. Gas station attendants do not welcome truckloads of Latin-American migrants as rest-room patrons.

The Texas Mexicans of the Southwest may be, by right of birth, American citizens of two or three or four generations. They may have journeyed oftener through more states than most traveling Americans manage to cross in a lifetime. But their ancient folkways stick. The influences of travel are negligible. Their horizon does not stretch or change; always its boundary remains the crop in which they work. The older ones speak only Spanish and read nothing; the younger ones have had a little schooling and they are functionally bilingual, but Spanish remains the language of the home.

There are valid reasons. Home base is near enough to Mexico so that travel back and forth is easy and common. In south Texas the custom persists in many families for the women to go to Mexico for their babies to be born. In towns of the border states the pattern of segregated living is traditional and entrenched.

Social scientists cite additional factors: pride in being Spanish, and a deep-rooted suspicion of Anglo-Americans. Such values as initiative, aggressiveness, and eager acceptance of change, they say, have low importance in Spanish folk culture; they are not traits to be cultivated. The *mañana* concept looms large; today the sun shines, let us enjoy it. This is a philosophy hardly conducive to systematic budgeting of time, to saving for a rainy day, to long-range planning. Yet if laziness were a concomitant of the Latin migrant character, growers in thirty-two states would scarcely recruit Texas Mexicans year after year to work for long hours in the hot sun at the hardest kind of physical labor.

To distinguish them from foreign workers, United States

citizens in the seasonal farm labor force are commonly described as "domestic." Of this domestic labor supply, the Fontanez family and other Spanish-speaking people from the Southwest constitute a rough 50 per cent. Who make up the other half?

3. GOOD-BY
TO THE DOG RUN:

The Grady Family

In the past two decades, there has developed
another clearly identified migratory group made
up almost exclusively of Negroes who have their
home base in Florida. Many of these are ex-
sharecroppers or their descendants from other
southern states.
    —*Migratory Labor in American Agriculture.*

Right now, for the fourth spring running, the Grady household is huddled in the back of a crew leader's truck heading for
Maryland and points north. Altogether the truck is carrying
twenty-seven people, all Negro; just seven of them are Gradys.
Counting Lottie, that is, they make seven. Last summer after
Princess Anne was born there were eight of them for a little
bit of time, and then Sharlene died. She just grabbed that
Orange Crush bottle and drank it down before anybody saw
her. It had kerosene in it. She was not quite two.

Henry and Addie Grady used to sharecrop in Georgia. When
they took off for Florida, Henry's niece Lottie—she was fourteen
and in the seventh grade—begged her father to say she could
join up with them. She didn't like it at home, didn't get on

with her stepmother, wanted to get away. Her father didn't know what might happen if he said no, so he said yes.

Of the Grady children the oldest is Roosevelt, a serious, thin, quick-moving little boy of nine. He is a reliable bean picker; he can make corn bread as good as Mamma's; he thinks the world and all of Princess Anne. At seven, Sister is as pretty as a kitten and something on the spoiled side because Papa can't help being too easy with her. Five-year-old Matthew has a clubfoot and a way of making music on a five-and-dime-store harmonica that is better than the radio to set your feet tapping. The baby was born in Maryland tomatoes on the eastern shore of the Chesapeake near the town of Princess Anne. Matthew said let's call her Tomato, and this was just about the only time Roosevelt ever spoke up loud and said no. With a pretty name like Princess Anne right there waiting, that's what they ought to call her, he declared, and they did. Matthew said, Roosevelt, won't you never, never learn to take a joke?

Bumping along in the dark of the Florida highway, Addie Grady found the broad side of the metal suitcase a solid seat if not a soft one. To be sure, she couldn't doze; she had to brace her feet wide apart to keep from sliding off (Princess Anne was asleep in her lap), and there was no way to rest her back. Maybe it was the tender way her spine felt in the truck that set her to thinking about that old rocking chair way off in Georgia, the one they kept out in the dog run, and how easy it was to your bones.

That dog run. Matthew always liked to hear her tell about it, and each time he would make her describe it to him all over again because he couldn't quite remember it. He was only a year old when they left Georgia, and of all the places they'd lived since, never once had they fallen into one with a dog run (migrant labor camps just don't come that way), a house in two parts like, with a roof over the whole thing and this open passage in the middle from front to back. The dog run was a fine sitting-out place, and Addie was comfortable there sitting in the rocking chair and picking a chicken. Four years now and she could still smell that last chicken, new-killed and warm. The times between seemed more like a blur, but not that day. It was Friday, a soft September Georgia day. Friday always was a day for bad things to happen. The minute Henry stepped in and she saw his shadow at her feet she had that feeling, and just as soon as she looked at him she knew, the way his shoulders sagged and his eye shifty-like.

"We got to go, don't we, Henry?" Flat out she said it to him, just like that. Henry nodded, and Addie went right on picking the chicken and by and by Henry told her in bits and pieces.

Mr. Wilson had put it off as long as he could, but now he plain had to tear down their house in the cotton field so the tractor could go straight through. Last spring he told them he couldn't keep them sharecropping for him any longer; times were changing, she knew that. Mr. Wilson just bought two more farms close by—no more mules, let the machines do the heavy work. But they could stay on for a spell in the little house, he said, and work for him every now and then chopping cotton and picking.

Through the summer Henry worked some in the sawmill six miles away but not steady, and the 1940 Dodge that carried him to work and back drank up gas like a cat laps cream. Still they'd made out, what with the chickens and the pigs and the goat and the sweet potatoes and collards growing out back. (Mr. Wilson wasn't like some, wanting every inch in cotton; he'd let you have a garden.) But now this looked like the end.

Addie finished picking the chicken and let it rest in her lap. She looked at Henry and looked at him and didn't say a word till he just had to look straight at her. Then she told him, maybe it's the end of living here, but it's not the end of the Gradys, indeed it's not. And then she said it right out. What about that card down there in the window of the general store?

Henry knew what she meant all right. Both of them had looked at that card, and they'd spelled it out, word by word. It was true they hadn't talked serious about it, but why did the Johnsons pack up and shove off just last week? Because they saw that card, that's why. Farm work some place in Florida there was, that's what it said, and it told a town and a man's name.

What if they had both of them lived all their two lives right within five miles of this dog run? Well, this wasn't the whole big earth, not by any means. The Pink Lily Baptist Church and the revivals and the Sons and Daughters of Esther suppers and meetings, visiting at the general store on Saturday nights, catfish fresh out of the brook and sometimes a rabbit . . . folks will still be folks no matter where the Lord decides they better live. It's a sure thing Florida can't be so different. . . .

Four years of it now, and they were really in a rut, a north-south rut straggling all the long way from Homestead, Florida, to a turn-around in a New York State beanfield and nowhere along the road to pull out and stay put. No going back to Georgia—that life was gone for sure, rocking chair and all. But somewhere, somehow, sometime they were going to have a regular home again all theirs twelve months in the year and steady work and steady schooling for the children and all things like that.

Addie didn't talk about this to Henry. She didn't talk about it to anybody at all except now and then to Roosevelt, but she surely did cherish that dream and she didn't intend to let it go. It made for fine ruminating during those night-long truck rides.

4. HOME IS WHERE THE CROPS ARE RIPE

. . . a lodge in a cucumber field . . .
—Isaiah 1:8.

It never occurred to Addie Grady or to Henry that the farm work in Florida would not be permanent year-round employment. Through that first winter they made out all right, working first out of Belle Glade in beans and potatoes and celery and so on; in February they went on down to Homestead for tomatoes. (They never did find the man whose name appeared on the card in the store window back in Georgia.) But when spring came, it seemed they had no choice at all except to join up with a crew and go on the season. Life did not fulfill Addie's prediction; things got to be different in many ways.

The Grady family experience follows a familiar pattern. Just as the major Latin-American spring migration has its source in Texas, so does a giant river of southern Negro families like the Gradys pour out of Florida. Up the eastern seaboard it flows through the Carolinas, a branch of it going off to Virginia's Shenandoah Valley. The main stream ferries the James River and toils up the eastern shore of the Chesapeake. The fruit and vegetable farms of Pennsylvania, New Jersey, and New York recruit thousands of these Negro families, and a few of them go all the way to Maine to pick up potatoes in Aroostook County.

Although Florida is their winter operating base, few east-coast adult migrants name Florida as their birthplace. More than half have come originally from Georgia and the others from a scattering of southern states, chiefly South Carolina, Alabama, Mississippi, and Arkansas. Overwhelmingly they come straight out of a rural background, with no work experience other than farming in between. Born of sharecropper parents, they have been tractored out of their livings as sharecroppers, tenants, or day laborers on farms. Of formal schooling they have had little, usually about five years, the women a fraction more than the men. For most of them migrancy has become a way of life; once in the migrant stream, it seems next to impossible to escape. They may have been following the crops for one, five, fifteen, or twenty years, sometimes longer.

Intermingling with the Negro and the Latin-American rivers are tributaries of southern mountain families from Kentucky, Tennessee, West Virginia, and the Carolinas. Arkansas, Missouri, and Oklahoma contribute a share of displaced small farmers. Workers from Puerto Rico swell the eastern stream, as in the West do reservation Indians.

The majority of all these groups migrate as families, but there are exceptions. Those Puerto Ricans who are contracted through the Puerto Rican Labor Department and flown over directly from their native sugar-cane fields leave their families at home. In northern states there is some recruiting of student groups from southern Negro colleges. There is a fair number of unattached men and some women. In the Far West these "singles" are often men who spend their winters in the skid rows of Portland or San Francisco or Seattle. A government study analyzing the Oregon migrant population includes a category of "Anglos without families"; it estimates that perhaps half of these are "winos," are apt to be fifty or older, are usually not

born and bred to farm life and dislike it, are better informed
than the family man about public affairs, work hard to stay
alive and have vague thoughts of buying some clothes and
finding a town job, are likable and human, troubled but cheerful. Their frequent travel medium is "The Friendly Southern
Pacific," the migrant's generic term for a free ride on a boxcar.

These are the general patterns. Yet to make precise predictions
about the composition of migrant farm-labor streams in a given
year is no safer than to generalize about the location of colors
in a kaleidoscope. Negro migrants are likely to appear in any
state; so are "Anglos," as the garden-variety Americans are commonly called to distinguish them from migrants of Latin ancestry. Arizona lists its migrants in numerical order as Latin
American, Anglo-American, Negro, Indian.

Early in the nineteen fifties some five thousand Texas Mexicans turned up in the reclaimed Everglades of Florida's Collier
County. There was an economic reason for this; native Mexicans were swarming illegally over the border by the hundred
thousand in order to work in cotton for ten and twenty cents an
hour. Even when domestic labor was desperate enough to work
for the same wages, growers preferred the "wetbacks" because
fear of apprehension by immigration authorities made them
docile workers. Consequently thousands of Texas Mexican
American citizens who had previously migrated within Texas
found their jobs usurped by wetbacks. This happened to the
Fontanezes. To hunt for work they were forced to join the already swollen interstate streams, and the streams found new
channels. Aggressive government action has now made the wetback almost an anachronism, but the increased out-migration
from Texas continues. Today with a degree of regularity some
Texas crews migrate to Louisiana, Mississippi, Alabama, Florida,
North Carolina, and Delaware.

It is not easy to pronounce with accuracy how many domestic

agricultural migrants there are in the United States. The usual definition of a migrant farm worker is one who travels beyond commuting distance to work in crops. If he works in a cannery or a freezing plant or a cotton gin, although he may travel with his family beyond commuting distance and therefore share the hardships of migrant living, he is not ordinarily counted officially as an agricultural worker—unless he works also in the fields. A crew may work in a dozen states in the course of a year and in several locations within states. This means that state totals inevitably include duplicates. On the other hand, state figures count only those who are processed through Farm Placement offices; they do not include "free wheelers"—those who find their own jobs. The New York State Farm Placement Director estimates that the proportion of free wheelers runs about 40 per cent.

All these complications make an infallible nose count an impossibility. Because the Bureau of Employment Security has to have some kind of working estimates it arrives at them like this: it requests the Farm Placement Office in each state to report the number of migrants on record as working on the date of peak employment during the year. Then it adds up these totals and comes up with a conservative guess of a round half million domestic migrant workers.

Actually an enumeration of the domestic migration gives little more than half of the picture of the migrant farm-labor force in the United States. In addition, thirty-eight states use a total of well over four hunded thousand imported workers. Most of these are Mexican nationals; a few thousand are British West Indian or Canadian; a few hundred are Japanese or Filipino.

Here is the way the government estimates for a given year look in rounded figures:

STATE	DOMESTIC MIGRANTS (Exclusive of dependents who travel but do not work)	FOREIGN WORKERS	TOTAL
Texas	96,000	137,000*	233,000
California	60,000	84,000*	144,000
Michigan	47,000	11,000	58,000
New York	28,000	600	28,600
Florida	25,000	10,000	35,000
Kansas	21,000	30	21,030
Oregon	20,000	400	20,400
Washington	18,000	50	18,050
North Carolina	14,000	none	14,000
Missouri	13,000	1,000	14,000
New Jersey	13,000	800	13,800
Maryland	13,000	50	13,050
Wisconsin	12,000	1,500	13,500
Oklahoma	11,000	none	11,000
Virginia	11,000	600	11,600
Colorado	10,000	5,700	15,700
Ohio	10,000	30	10,000
Arkansas	9,000	39,000*	48,000
Idaho	9,000	none	9,000
Arizona	8,000	16,000*	24,000
Illinois	7,500	500	8,000
Pennsylvania	7,500	none	7,500
North Dakota	7,000	50	7,050
Montana	7,000	2,000	9,000
Indiana	7,000	1,500	8,500
Minnesota	5,000	300	5,300
Georgia	5,000	1,000	6,000
Louisiana	5,000	none	5,000
Delaware	5,000	none	5,000
Connecticut	4,500	1,200	5,700
Nebraska	4,000	2,000	6,000
South Carolina	3,500	none	3,500
Kentucky	3,500	350	3,850
Alabama	3,500	none	3,500
Utah	2,500	400	2,900

* These five states use four fifths of the Mexican nationals.

STATE	DOMESTIC MIGRANTS (Exclusive of dependents who travel but do not work)	FOREIGN WORKERS	TOTAL
Wyoming	2,000	1,200	3,200
South Dakota	2,000	200	2,200
Massachusetts	1,500	500	2,000
New Mexico	1,500	20,000*	21,500
Mississippi	1,500	none	1,500
Iowa	800	75	875
Nevada	600	100	700
West Virginia	600	400	1,000
Tennessee	500	800	1,300
Maine	400	8,100	8,500
New Hampshire	300	200	500
Vermont	200	25	225

* These five states use four fifths of the Mexican nationals.

Three states do not appear in this list: Alaska, Hawaii, and Rhode Island. In actual fact, some migrants do work in Rhode Island potatoes during summer and fall, and some thirty Puerto Ricans are employed in nurseries from March to November. They are not reported because there are fewer than one hundred at work in any one day.

In the tabulation of foreign workers there are two points of interest. First, they add up to fewer than the actual number imported nationally during the calendar year; the reason is that the figures represent only those at work on a single day in a given state. Second, although foreign workers appear in thirty-eight states, four fifths of them are concentrated in just five states: Texas, California, Arkansas, Arizona, and New Mexico.

Add to these domestic and foreign totals an undetermined number of free wheelers and another undetermined number of non-working dependents traveling with their families, and it becomes all too clear that a million is a rock-bottom figure for the number of people in the United States to whom, for the better part of the year, home is wherever the crops are ripe; or as a little migrant boy put it when asked where he lived, "I live wherever we're at."

5.   WHAT KIND
OF PEOPLE?

> I believe in aristocracy . . . Not an aristocracy
> of power, based upon rank and influence, but
> an aristocracy of the sensitive, the considerate
> and the plucky. Its members are to be found in
> all nations and classes, and all through the ages,
> and there is a secret understanding between
> them when they meet . . . They represent the
> true human tradition, the one permanent victory
> of our queer race over cruelty and chaos. Thou-
> sands of them perish in obscurity . . .
>
> —*E. M. Forster.*

As a facet of American life, agricultural migrancy has characteristics peculiarly its own.

The migrant is a minority within a minority. The components of the general migrant population belong to racial or ethnic minorities. In addition, each in turn within his own ethnic group occupies a place at the very bottom of the social and economic hierarchy. He meets the most discrimination, does the hardest work, earns the least money; he has the least job security, the least formal schooling, the lowest status. His migrancy separates him from the larger community; his minority status aggravates the separation.

Migrancy is unobtrusive. It lacks the visibility of large-scale

housing developments or city slums. Neither its erstwhile barns
and hen houses nor its barrack compounds nor yet its newer
cinder-block housing units stand near the superhighways. In its
trekking migrancy does not frequent toll roads. Unlike suburbia,
it imposes no patterns of living on the national culture; its way
of life does not invite imitation.

The migrant works in a labor market that, in spite of years of
well-intentioned and zealous effort of public and private agencies and individuals, can only be described as chaotic. He is a
necessary cog in an agricultural machine that differs from the
traditional family farm in just about the same degree that the
shop of the village blacksmith differs from a General Motors
assembly line. The urban influences that tend to lift the material
level of living of the rest of the American community have been
slow to penetrate his rural folk culture. He has little or no
education. He is unorganized and inarticulate; there is no
indigenous leadership to speak in his behalf. The stoop labor
he performs makes the most severe demands on his physical
stamina, yet he is not regarded as belonging to labor with a
capital "L." If the cotton he picks is deliberately weighed short,
he has no legal recourse. His grievance does not fall within the
jurisdiction of a labor relations board. The protections of the
Fair Labor Standards Act do not extend to him. The forces of
industrial labor have tried to organize migrant farm workers;
the results have been negligible. If labor legislation and aca-
demic treatises on labor mention farm workers at all, they do so
only to specify that agriculture is excluded from consideration.
Sensing exploitation, the migrant may bite back, but his bite is
sporadic, illogical, and futile. And his teeth are weak. In an
industrial economy he stands as a lonely anachronism.

Migrancy engenders community resentment, puts in peril
such practical aspects of normal family living as regular schooling for children, housing that is sanitary and convenient and

conducive to wholesome family relationships, voting privileges, stable income, health and welfare services available to residents. Migrancy reduces to zero the chance to develop the feeling of belonging to a stable community.

Time and again the cumulative negatives surrounding migrancy break through to fascinate and appall the public conscience; but as they haunt it, they also confound it. The public does not know what to do about them. The thorny questions they raise generate strong feelings, but they neither win nor lose elections. Faced with pressures from powerful farm groups and dwarfed by larger issues, they simply stay lost.

What kind of people choose a way of life with so many disadvantages? And why do they do it? Are they just too happy-go-lucky to hold down a steady job in one locale? Or are they too lazy? How accurate is the stereotype of itchy feet?

If it is difficult to make definitive pronouncements about numbers of migrant workers and their migration patterns, it is even more hazardous to generalize about the motivations, the habits, the values, the behavior and culture patterns either of migrants across the board or of the individual groups that make up this fluid, massive, leaderless army. It is an easy pitfall to blunder into accepting the caricature of the irresponsible Mexican, the volatile Puerto Rican, the razor-carrying Negro, the feud-holding mountaineer, the lazy Indian, the drunken stumble-bum and to forget that individual differences of temperament and talent exist within all groups.

The truth is that all sorts of people turn up as migrants: people frail and solid, perceptive and dull, industrious and indolent, sensitive and stoic, crusty and charming, honest and crooked, clean and dirty. To attribute particular motivations to them and to predict their behavior in special situations is just as inaccurate as it is with businessmen or schoolteachers or lawyers or politicians or farmers.

At the same time, along with disposition and native ability, group mores and the limitations of environment do operate to determine how individuals respond to recurring situations. Annunciata Fontanez is governed by standards of behavior traditional for Mexican women. Negroes with generations of plantation culture behind them share a casual attitude toward time not found among Negroes with long-time urban experience. Reservation Indian people exhibit tribal loyalties difficult for Anglos to comprehend.

Apart from ethnic differences, the very nature of migrancy makes it possible to isolate certain values and social characteristics commonly found among migrants: a spirit of resignation; a sense of being trapped; an astonishing lack of bitterness; a fierce family loyalty; a buoyant, often subtle wit; a tendency to spend money, when they have it, to meet not only immediate needs but immediate desires; a longing to be somebody, manifested sometimes as a blatant groping for status, more often as a craving for recognition as a human being; a longing for a better life for their children; a quick and generous sympathy for neighbors in trouble; a high incidence of stamina and courage.

In all the migrating groups there are a few who like the freedom to move about; there are a few who simply like to work outdoors; there are some who enjoy the independence of working at a piece rate and stopping when they feel inclined. Especially with the southwestern Latin workers the element of excitement at the prospect of a trip north plays a part. The fact that crops give opportunity for every member of the family to earn money figures as a strongly persuasive factor.

But with due allowance for the part played by all these motivations, for overwhelming numbers migration offers the only visible alternative to unemployment. There is at the heart of the "why" question one categorical answer. Unlike restlessness or improvidence or sloth, its key is neither a native characteristic nor an acquired mode of behavior. It is an external factor, a pressure from environment. It is primitive and it is stark.

Asked where he secured his seasonal workers, the personnel director of an industrial farm on the eastern seaboard said:

"I tell you, I've been in this business for twenty-eight years. Back in the thirties we used day hauls from the cities; you know, Italians and Polocks and Hunkies and people like that. In the early forties we had prisoners of war, and sometimes we've contracted for British West Indians. These past years we've had Negro families from the South and some Puerto Ricans, sugar-cane workers off the Island. They change as the years go by, but I'll tell you one thing for sure. When spring comes, whoever they are, they're the people who are the hungriest. Who else wants to work that hard for that little money?"

Well, who does?

Like the southern Negroes, most of the migrating Anglo families come from a hand-to-mouth existence, either as displaced tenants or sharecroppers or as marginal farm owners unable to meet the competition of mechanized agriculture. Some have made abortive attempts to work in industry, but with little education and few skills, they are the inevitable first victims of layoffs.

Jim Vinson worked in a score of states after the summer ten years back when he first took his child-wife and their baby girl Lucy from their Kentucky hill farm to pick blueberries in Michigan.

Two thirds of Jim's eighty Kentucky acres were untillable wooded upland, and his cash intake in a good year never came to more than a thousand dollars. When Lucy was born, Ellie

Vinson was fifteen; she had a difficult confinement. Jim's meager savings stretched to cover only a fifth of the hospital bill. Ellie's brother lent money to pay the rest. Jim Vinson had been bred to a horror of debt even within the family, and migration to a place where he and Ellie both could work for cash looked like a good, and indeed the only, way to pay off the loan.

As she picked, Ellie would park Lucy at the end of each blueberry row. By the close of the second summer in Michigan, Jim was able to pay off his brother-in-law's loan. But the following spring Kentucky floods wiped out all his crops. It was too late to replant, and this time they went to Arkansas. From there to Oklahoma. Then to Idaho.

They never did get back to Kentucky, and Ellie never did grow up. Each year brought a new baby, and with each addition to the family Ellie receded further into childhood. She grew physically robust; she was docile, and she worked in the fields without complaint, but she seldom spoke and she made no attempt to cope with her family. By the time Lucy was ten, it was not her mother but Lucy who cooked the eternal grits and hot dogs and macaroni and Jello, did the washing, and more or less looked after her seven brothers and sisters, rounding them up and counting them when Jim said it was time to move on.

As for Jim, he worked doggedly whenever and wherever there was work to be had. A few times he tried to get work at something besides picking. He was strong, but he had no experience at anything but farming and he had no facility for selling himself. Once they found out that he was a migrant, employers of day labor shook their heads. For five days in Indiana he did get work replacing railroad ties, and then the job folded. After that he stopped trying for any kind of work but crops. Every time he was paid, the first three dollars went into his right shoe. No matter if crops were running good or bad, and even when the picking kept him working ten hours a day for seven days in the week, each Saturday night he religiously took the three dollars out of his right shoe, found a tavern in the nearest town, and quietly and systematically got drunk.

Most isolated from the general American community are the Indian migrant workers. On most reservations jobs are scarce and cash is a rare commodity. For years Arizona has used Navahos in carrots, onions, radishes, and cotton in Maricopa County; Apaches in cotton at Safford; and Papagos, Pimas, and Yumas in cotton, vegetables, and cantaloupes in the Salt River Valley. Utah counts on Navahos and Hopis from Arizona and New Mexico for spring cultivation and thinning and for fall harvest of vegetables, fruit, and sugar beets. Reservation Indians in South Dakota spurn sugar-beet work in their own state, but they will travel to Colorado to do it. A number of other states depend to a degree on Indian labor: Washington, Oregon, California, Texas, Oklahoma, Idaho, Iowa, Wisconsin, North Carolina.

For ten years the Yazzie family have been part of a crew of some fifty Navahos who work each winter for an onion grower north of Phoenix. Some of the families migrate several times during the year, but so far the winter onion season is the only time the Yazzies make a mass exodus, departing from their windowless hogan with its smoke hole in the top and its doorway facing the east, and taking with them their blankets and their goatskins for comfortable sleeping.

Ben Yazzie, now sixteen, stays behind to tend the family sheep; Irene, fourteen, attends the government Indian boarding school in Phoenix; and twenty-one-year-old Melvin is off in Los Angeles working in an airplane plant. Everybody else goes on the onions; this year there are nine of them, from the ancient great-grandmother to the baby in the cradleboard.

The Yazzies could ride in the bus that the grower sends to Window Rock to collect his workers, but they prefer to go the whole distance in their own pickup truck in order to be able to take a day off from onions and drive into Phoenix to visit Irene.

The frosty Monument Valley winter in northeastern Arizona can be a lean and hungry time. One year a blizzard cut off the Yazzie hogan from the trading post for five weeks; they were kept from starving by bundles of flour and dried meat and powdered milk and cheese dropped by army planes; hay was sent down the same way for the sheep. It was when the thaw came after this experience that the Yazzies first migrated to the onion fields. Now the 250-mile trek has become an annual event.

In the fields the cradleboard keeps the baby safe, and as he grows big enough to crawl, an onion crate doubles as a playpen. The grandmother and the great-grandmother do not work in the fields; they spend the days in camp sitting on the ground in their flowing skirts, the jewel-bright green and gold of their velvet basque blouses glowing in the sunshine. With patient care they cut off onion tops, gather the young green onions into bundles, and fasten them with rubber bands. Every now and then a truck makes the rounds in the camp to collect the tidy bundles and the discarded tops and to deliver a new supply of onions to be topped and sorted.

The onion grower likes his Navahos. He knows they are slow workers, but he knows, too, that they are painstaking, that they follow directions meticulously. He understands that they do not respond to the incentive of competition but do work well as a group. He accepts philosophically the reality that a sing or a corn dance, a camp meeting or a family crisis will inevitably take precedence over job responsibility.

The money the Yazzies earn from onions insures a steady supply of dried meat and corn meal and canned peaches and coffee from the trading post, keeps the truck in gas and oil and tires, buys jeans and shirts and hats for the men and yard goods for the women, enables Irene to shop in Phoenix stores for sweaters and skirts, ankle socks and loafers. Last year their earnings bought two luxuries: a treadle sewing machine and a battery radio. A family consultation resulted in the decision to leave the radio at home this winter to keep Ben company on his lonely vigil with the sheep.

Since 1917 Puerto Ricans have been American citizens; consequently stateside Puerto Rican migrants are counted as domestic. Yet many of them work under conditions different from those of other domestic labor. Those who come under the sponsorship of the Puerto Rican Labor Department enjoy a number of protections unique among domestic migrants: a written contract; a guarantee of 160 hours of work for each four-week period at the prevailing wage; written statements of hours worked and earnings; workmen's compensation; individual bed or cot, mattress, water, light, and fuel, all supplied without charge; either three adequate meals per day at a specified minimum cost or cooking and eating facilities provided at no cost to the worker; group health insurance toward which both employers and workers contribute.

The Puerto Rican Labor Department specifies that "the worker shall not be subject to discrimination in employment, housing or any other regard because of race, color, creed, membership in or activity in behalf of any labor organization." As a result of this condition, there has been no contracting of Puerto Rican workers throughout the South, where assurance of freedom from community discrimination cannot be given; Puerto Ricans generally are classed with Negroes. Nevertheless, substantial numbers of them are found working all the way from Delaware to Florida. Some come first under contract to work in New Jersey or Pennsylvania or New York, and when fall comes, instead of returning home immediately, decide to work their way south or to take a Florida vacation. Others, stimulated by information from relatives or friends, fly directly from the Island to Florida, sometimes with their families, and find work as free-wheelers; these are the "walk-ins."

In the North increasing numbers are bringing in their families and settling down; little colonies are growing along the shores of Lake Erie from Lorain through Ashtabula and on up toward Buffalo. Their aim, they will tell you, is to learn enough English to get a job in a *factoría* and make a new life for themselves and their children. Meantime they work in fruit in the summer and at odd jobs in the winter.

Overpopulation and underemployment at home plus a stateside farm-labor shortage in 1947 prompted the initiation of the contract program, and in 1948 a modest 2382 were flown in and contracted to eastern-seaboard growers. On the Island the slack season in sugar cane coincides with stateside peak harvest needs in the northeast. Cutting asparagus in New Jersey is hard work, but it cannot match the grueling labor of swinging a machete to cut heavy stalks of sugar cane under a tropical sun. The Puerto Ricans like to come; the little country post offices in the centers where they work do a booming money-order business as they send their earnings to their families back home. New Jersey records that in a single season 7702 Puerto Ricans under contract earned $3,546,000. Each year now sees ten to fifteen thousand under contract and unknown numbers of walk-ins.

Those who do not work under contract suffer the same disadvantages as other domestic workers. When employers bypass the Puerto Rican Labor Department and get in touch directly with workers on the Island whom they have previously employed under contract, there is no machinery to insure the workers the continuing protections of specified wages, guaranteed hours of work, minimum housing standards, or insurance coverage. Two Puerto Ricans recruited in this way to spray crops in Massachusetts died from contact with poisonous insecticide. They were not covered by insurance, and their families received no compensation.

Puerto Rican migrants are a young group. Felipe Ovieto was twenty-three when he first arrived at the Garden State Co-operative Camp at Glassboro, New Jersey. His two summers in the United States have been a satisfactory experience, and he hopes to return. In Puerto Rico, on his own two stony mountainside acres, he and his wife Cristina raise pole beans, corn, sweet potatoes, tomatoes, and pimientos; they have a goat, some rather scrawny hens, one rooster, and one fighting cock. Each winter Felipe gets three months' work cutting sugar cane, earning about three hundred dollars; this is the total of their annual cash intake. That first summer in New Jersey he worked on a number of different farms, mainly in asparagus, tomatoes, and apples. The following season he came again under contract to the Co-operative, but this time he worked straight through the season for the same grower, a nurseryman. The nursery was fifteen miles from the Glassboro camp. Each morning Mr. Beach, the owner, drove over to get Felipe and drove him back each evening. In the course of the season Felipe planted, cultivated, cut, and packed Christmas trees. He sent home ten dollars a week, and when he flew back to the Island in the fall, he took with him a hundred dollars of savings and a guitar.

"Mr. Beach likes me," he told Cristina. "I know he likes me. You see, he gave me the guitar."

The Foreign Worker

6. FLOWER BED:
THE ADVENTURE OF ARMANDO

> In the United States, they told us, you sweep
> the dollars with a broom.
> —*Alphonso Martinez, who came to the United
> States as a wetback in 1946 and is now a student
> at Asbury College in Wilmore, Kentucky.*

Armando Santiago began his adventure on the back of a
burro.

He wore white cotton pants and a white shirt. A bright blue
serape draped his shoulders; it was fringed, and through the
center ran narrow stripes of red and green and gold. On his
head sat a broad-brimmed hat of straw. The edges rolled slightly
up on either side; the crown was peaked. He wore *huarachos*
on his feet. A tote bag of rainbow straw, dyed and woven by
Rosa, his wife, carried extra clothing and enough *tortillas*, fried
black beans, rice, and coffee in a goatskin flask to see him
through the two-day journey to the bus stop.

The burro belonged to his father. According to agreement,
Armando would leave the burro with his uncle, who ran a
cantina beside the market in Chalingo. There he would board
the bus that would take him the long thousand miles north to

Monterrey. The uncle would keep the burro until the nephew came back from his adventure.

Armando was not happy about his expedition. He had high cheekbones, full lips, and gentle eyes, a straight back and a tough and wiry body, but neither his face nor his demeanor spoke the exhilaration that should attend the beginning of an exciting journey. Under the great hat the face looked sad and vulnerable; under the serape the young shoulders drooped. The truth was, Armando suffered from shyness; the unfamiliar filled him with dread. In all his twenty-six years only once before had he been more than seventy-five miles from home, and that was when he had to work out his period of service with the Mexican Army. The recollection shook him with the panic of nightmare; the whole time he was acutely, desperately homesick, bitterly ashamed of being homesick, mortified at his dislike of the military life, living for the day when it should end.

At home in Mesa Pequeña with Rosa and their two brown children—Rosita, an angel of four, and Pepe, an energetic two —Armando felt safe and contented. As a *campesino*, a day laborer in the fields, he earned (when there was work to be had) four, six, eight, sometimes ten pesos a day, never so much as a United States dollar. The money bought salt and matches and masses, dress goods and machetes and Coca-Cola and lottery tickets. Nobody in Mesa Pequeña had an automobile, a refrigerator, a bathroom, a tractor, a television set; everybody had—or could have if he wanted to bother—mangos and bananas and maize and mulberries and *garbanzos* and tobacco and coffee and goats and pigs and chickens and ducks.

Armando and his family lived in a one-room adobe hut with a dirt floor and a palmetto-thatched roof. Armando built it himself on a corner of his father's land. Inside, four ropes converging to a hook in the roof suspended a flat, oblong hammock of wood; here the children slept. There were a straw pallet, a stone charcoal brazier, and two wooden storage chests. On one wall hung a crucifix bought at the Chalingo market and a wedding certificate, on another a tattered airline travel poster brought back from El Paso by Armando's brother Rafael, showing a little Dutch girl in a blaze of gold and crimson tulips.

In no way was the hut itself very different from that of any of the other two hundred residents of Mesa Pequeña. What gave distinction to the home was Rosa's flower bed. In a plot beside the door, marked off by a brush fence to keep out the ducks and pigs, it flamed, an uninhibited glory of calendulas, geraniums, calla lilies, camellias, poppies, sunflowers. No other garden flourished with anything like the abandon of Rosa's; it was the pride of the family and the pride of the village.

On evenings and Sundays and fiesta days the people walked in the plaza, gossiped and sang and quarreled and danced to guitars and tambours and *jaranas,* gambled and wrestled and fought with knives and drank pulque and mescal and tequila and went to cockfights and went to church. When sickness struck there were *curanderos* to give counsel or encouragement; to exorcise ghosts; to administer eucalyptus for heart trouble, powdered rice for fever, and ant weed for appendicitis. *Parteras* delivered the children; they knew how to stimulate mother's milk with mint. All of it went to make up a world Armando knew, a world where he belonged.

Never would he have started out on this trip had it not been for family pressure. The pressure came from his mother and father, and back of it all was his older brother Rafael. Armando idolized Rafael, bluff and swaggering with his boisterous jokes and his generous gestures, favorite of all the village girls and many of the wives. (But not of Rosa; for Rafael, Rosa had no time at all.)

From childhood Rafael displayed an impatient affection for Armando, protecting him at the same time that he egged him on to attempt feats beyond his strength.

Rafael had been many times across the Rio Grande, first as

a wetback, later as a bracero, a worker under contract. The last time he brought back with him a bride, Josefina, a city girl from Juarez. A hard piece and an odd one, the neighbors said, not gay and giving like Rafael. Why did he marry her? And as to that, why did she marry him? Charm he had, but he was no great catch. It was a mystery.

With his earnings from the cotton in the United States, Rafael bought some land and set up a chicken ranch.

Always when he came back to the village from the United States, Rafael had tried without success to uproot Armando. After he married Josefina and settled down on his chicken ranch he adopted a new strategy. He worked not on Armando but on their mother and father.

"The United States, it is a paradise," he would tell them. His details of what life there was like were generally vague, but on two points they were explicit. When his father asked him in what way precisely it was a paradise, he would say:

"The work—there's work to be had—and the money. In just two hours you earn a day of Mexican wages. It is unbelievable. Me, the money drips from my fingers; three trips it has taken me to save enough for my chicken ranch. But Armando with his thrifty ways, in six weeks he could earn enough to rent twenty acres in the valley and work it for the patrón on shares, keeping seventy-five per cent of the profit. He is a fool, that one, not to take the chance."

By nature Armando was the most amiable of men. He abhorred dissension; he liked to acquiesce, to please. When even Rosa added her voice to the chorus, he could hold out no longer.

"Go," she said. "Go and see for yourself this paradise, if the work and the money are as he says. To me it sounds not sensible. More like the truth, he stole the money for his chicken ranch. But go, go and find out. Then we shall know."

Terrified though he was of the strange world outside Mesa Pequeña, his reluctance to persist in crossing the entire family, coupled with the need to justify Rafael to Rosa, these won out over his apprehension.

So it was that he found himself on the back of his father's burro headed for the bus stop, a two-day jog trot from home, in his pocket a hundred pesos given him by Rafael to cover the cost of his trip north. (A moneylender would have charged him interest at 10 per cent a month, this he knew; Rafael did not even say, "Sometime, sometime you pay me back." Rafael had a great heart.)

Rafael made all the arrangements, slipping a *mordida* of a hundred pesos here and a hundred there into the proper hands and returning with a *permiso* from the *Presidente Municipal* stating that Armando Santiago, a qualified unemployed farm worker and a reliable man, had completed his military service for the Mexican Government and was hereby certified to apply to the United States Immigration authorities for contract farm labor in the United States.

Arriving in Chalingo, Armando left the burro with his uncle at the cantina, had his picture taken and fastened to his *permiso,* and for sixty-five of his hundred pesos bought a third-class bus ticket to Monterrey. On the bus he found nineteen other men headed for the same destination. The trip took three days and three nights. Armando enjoyed talking to the other men, and they had a good time on the bus. It was Friday midnight when they reached Monterrey. Armando and two companions from the bus did not try to find beds to sleep in; they did not want to spend the money. They simply holed up in the brush outside of town until Saturday morning. Then they found that the migratory center was closed over the weekend. They bought tamales and beans and coffee in tiny shops along the railroad track and passed the time wandering through the city, returning to the brush to sleep.

On Monday morning outside a tall fence at the migratory center they found themselves in a throng of braceros from all over Mexico; three thousand, one man said. Armando began to feel uneasy in his serape, his white work pants, and his huarachos. Many of the men wore blue jeans, shirts in patterns of large loud checks, and cowboy boots. These men came, he found, from the north of Mexico.

Armed guards had the men arrange themselves in groups according to their home localities, and gradually and in an orderly way they were admitted through a gate in the fence into a yard. Here an official spoke to them in Spanish over a loud-speaker, calling off each man's name from a list. It seemed to be a mass operation very like the army, and as the hours passed it became more so. Armando felt his identity slipping away from him; he descended into a trance, like an automaton keeping his place in the line, speaking only when spoken to, doing as he was bidden.

During the next thirty-six hours he answered questions (What crops have you worked? Let me see your hands. Have you ever been in jail? What organizations do you belong to?); stripped and allowed himself to be tested for heart, lung, and venereal disease, vaccinated for smallpox, fingerprinted, dusted with DDT; ate (with no sensation of taste) a hearty lunch of hot, rich stew, beans, bread, and coffee; accepted a packet of meat sandwiches; rode for six hours in a bus across the border to Hidalgo, Texas; spent the night in the barracks at the United States reception center; answered more questions very like the others; submitted to a second physical examination minus the vaccination but including the DDT; was passed by the Immigration Inspector because his name did not appear on a list of inadmissible aliens; found himself one of three hundred men selected by the recruiting officer of a Texas growers' association; put his fingerprint at the end of an impressive contract printed in Spanish and English; listened to but understood little of an explanation of the contract; was given a copy of the contract and a booklet in Spanish entitled *Guía para los Trabajadores Agrícolas Mexicanos en los Estados Unidos de Norte América* (neither of which he could read, to be sure, because he could read scarcely anything at all); boarded a bus and traveled fifty miles to a labor camp run by the growers' association.

Armando had no way of knowing that his contract gave him assurances of protection unknown to domestic migrants. It specified hygienic lodgings with bed or cot, mattress, and blanket when necessary; full employment for three weeks out of every four; payment of not less than fifty cents an hour or its equivalent at piecework rates with normal diligence, or more if the prevailing wage was higher; three meals a day at no more than $1.75 a day or, if Armando should so choose, cooking facilities and a food allowance; occupational insurance paid for by the employer; life and health insurance paid by deductions from Armando's earnings; the right to vote for a representative to be recognized by the employer as a spokesman for the workers.

Once in the fields, Armando came to life and began to enjoy himself. Although the onions, carrots, radishes, broccoli, and cotton were crops in which he had not worked before, it was not difficult to learn what to do. He worked all told on twenty different farms, always at the prevailing piecework rates. Because these changed from crop to crop and sometimes from day to day, and because he did not understand the deductions (something called a *bonus*, for instance, seemed often to be taken out; this, a friend explained, was a part of his earnings held back until the end of his contract period to make sure that he would stay on the job according to his agreement), he never knew what his earnings would amount to, but he liked the element of surprise connected with his pay. Some of the men grumbled and complained that they were not being paid the right amount, but the word soon spread that the foreman did not like to be asked questions about the pay and had even threatened to have the grumblers sent back to Mexico.

One man insisted that he be given a stove to cook his own meals. This the foreman told him would not be practical; it was ten miles to town, and how could he walk there after a day's work to buy provisions and come back and prepare himself a healthy meal and have his strength for work the next day?

One evening a week the camp manager arranged that all who desired to go be taken to town in buses for shopping. With his first earnings Armando bought himself tan work pants, an American-style harvest hat, and heavy brown sport shoes with thick ridged crepe-rubber soles. From then on his great preoccupation on the evenings in town was wandering from store to store, planning what gifts he would take back to Mesa Pequeña. One special present for Rosa he bought as soon as he saw it because he was so sure it was right: an outsize striped umbrella with a long handle to fix in the ground beside the flower bed and cast shade.

Evenings and days when there was no work in the fields time hung heavy. Hearing in the morning that there would be no work, the men would say, "Today we count the flies." They played cards, or somebody would start a ball game, or somebody would bring out a guitar and they would sing old Mexican songs and make up new ones. A large sign at the entrance to the camp forbade trespassers, and there were no visitors. The only Americans Armando talked with were the foremen and the row bosses in the fields and the clerks in the stores; they usually spoke a little Spanish and he picked up a few words of English and got along. He did not get drunk and he had no brush with the police.

Many of the men, he found, sent home money orders to their families. The foreman took care of this for them, but he charged them two dollars for each money order, a wanton expense, Armando thought. Since neither he nor Rosa nor his parents could write a letter or even read one, he had no communication of any kind with Mesa Pequeña during his absence.

He was gone for six months.

He saved a hundred and sixty dollars, nearly thirteen hundred pesos.

It was a new Armando, a figure of triumph, erect and beaming, who rode the burro into Mesa Pequeña late one afternoon. Gone were the serape, the sombrero, the huarachos; in their stead, a canvas windbreaker, a shirt of lemon yellow, pants of a soft blue color, the American-style harvest hat, and the sport shoes with the ridged crepe-rubber soles. One hand held upright over his head the beach umbrella, raised to show its full glory. Rolled up in the rainbow straw bag along with his discarded clothes were the family presents: Rosita's doll, Pepe's cowboy suit, the red shoes with spike heels for Rosa, the earrings for his mother, the shirt for his father and the shirt for Rafael, the scarf for Josefina.

No one was about as he passed his father's place; he shouted, but there was no reply. The lane turned just here and his inward eye filled with a picture of the vision he was about to see, the riot of red and gold and white that was Rosa's flower bed. So real was the picture in his mind that when he reached his own house he could not credit what he saw: the flower bed a mockery, weedy, dry, desolate, no bloom in sight, only shriveling leaves and ghostly stalks; the brush fence a mass of devastation; and profanely sleeping in the middle of the ruin—a sow.

He let the umbrella slip from his grasp; it bounced awkwardly on the ground toward the wasted flower bed. He slid from the burro and ran into the hut, his cries of "Rosa, Rosa" like a lost child's, mounting to panic. The hut was empty, clean, without life. The stone brazier, the hammock, the straw pallet, the two chests, the crucifix, the little Dutch girl in the tulips, everything was there, everything in its place. Except for one thing. The wedding certificate was gone.

For what happened while Armando was away his mother blamed Josefina.

"She was a bad one. So she did not like the chicken ranch, so she should not have married Rafael in the first place. To marry him and then run away, this was not right."

Armando's father blamed Rafael.

"That Rafael with his great tongue. He made Josefina think he was bringing her to a palace to live with a prince. It shames me that he should be my son."

The women of the village blamed Rosa.

"She had no right to take up with Rafael. Her place it was to wait at home with her children. No matter how long."

Confidentially among themselves the young girls whispered their envy of Rosa.

"That Rafael, how could she resist him!"

Nobody blamed Armando; indeed, he took on new stature in the village eyes as a man of passion. Did he not, for love of his wife, with a single blow between the eyes, a blow with the beach umbrella, kill the sow in the flower bed?

7. THE VAMPIRE BAT

> And I might say that I personally, in the presence of others who were with me on the trip into the field, talked to a very prominent grower who, when I asked him what he thought about Public Law 78, said, "Well, it is not as good as the wetbacks." He said, "The ideal situation was when we had the wetbacks, but if we cannot have the wetbacks, for God's sake do not take Public Law 78 away from us."
> —*Rt. Rev. Msgr. George G. Higgins, National Catholic Welfare Conference.*

During five days of March in 1960, in a committee room in the House of Representatives Office Building in Washington, the Subcommittee on Agriculture conducted hearings on this deceptively simple-sounding issue:

Should or should not the Congress of the United States authorize the continuing importation of contract farm labor from Mexico?

The wire services carried little word on this show, yet a good many people were, it seemed, for one reason or another exercised about it. In addition to the questioning and testimony of sixty-odd witnesses, many of them representing membership organizations, the 429-page printed record presents ninety-four items of other data: statements, tables, charts, letters, telegrams, local newspaper features and editorials. Even as congressional hearings go, this is a fair amount of bulk for a five-day accumulation on an obscure and specialized subject that seems to affect only a small segment of the population. Furthermore, these were not the first hearings held by this committee on the question. Two years earlier, in June 1958, it listened to arguments for and against; as a result, the enabling legislation known as Public Law 78 was extended by Congress for two years. And this had happened twice before, at two-year intervals. The 1958 congressional action brought to June 1961 the termination date of Public Law 78, with recognition of the fact that this would mean reopening the issue in an election year.

As a consequence, in March 1960, with the expiration date of Public Law 78 fifteen months away, once again the battle lines were drawn.

On the affirmative side there were present articulate representatives from the American Farm Bureau Federation and the National Grange, plus a battery of spokesmen for certain large agricultural organizations:

National Cotton Council

> The over-all organization of the raw cotton industry, consisting of cotton producers, ginners, merchants, warehousemen, spinners, and cotton-seed crushers in the nineteen cotton-producing states. Headquarters, Memphis, Tenn.

National Beet Growers Federation

> Eighteen affiliates in eleven states. Headquarters, Greeley, Colorado.

Amalgamated Sugar Company

> Covers a territory with 6000 growers of sugar beets; in 1959 the

company contracted 90,000 acres of sugar beets in Idaho, Oregon, and Utah.

National Farm Labor Users Committee
1150 members.

National Council of Farmer Co-operatives
Membership made up of marketing associations.

Vegetable Growers Association of America
Forty-nine affiliated associations with membership in thirty states.

Agricultural Council of Arkansas

Ventura County Citrus Growers Committee (California)

Imperial Valley Farmers Association (California)

Lower Rio Grande Valley Ginners Association (Texas)

Artesia Alfalfa Growers Association (New Mexico)

Michigan Field Crops, Inc.
For thirty years has had an extensive recruiting organization in Texas.

Opponents generally fell into one of two categories, the representatives of organized labor:

AFL-CIO

Agricultural Workers Organizing Committee

Industrial Union Department

United Packing House Workers

National Agricultural Workers Union

Amalgamated Meat Cutters and Butcher Workmen

Textile Workers Union of America

Joint United States-Mexico Trade Union Committee:
United States Section

and six agencies concerned with human rights and social reform, including both Roman Catholic and Protestant church groups:

National Consumers League

National Sharecroppers Fund

National Advisory Committee on Farm Labor

National Federation of Settlements and Neighborhood Centers

National Council of Churches

National Catholic Welfare Conference

As usual at congressional hearings, organizations not represented in person registered opinion by letter or wire. In the case of the social agencies, groups were heard from with names like:

The Opportunity Council, Inc.
  Organizations and individuals in northern Cook County, Illinois, interested in American citizens of Mexican descent.

Community Service Organization (California)

American GI Forum
  Veterans organization composed chiefly of people of Mexican origin: organized in twenty-three states; headquarters in Texas.

California Citizens Committee of Agricultural Labor

Consumers League of New York

Consumers League of New Jersey

National Child Labor Committee

National Association for the Advancement of Colored People

Workers Defense League

American Friends Service Committee

Committee on Migrant Farm Labor of the Palo Alto Unitarian Church

Minnesota Council of Churches

Catholic Bishops of Wisconsin

There is no indication that during the five days of hearings anybody converted anybody else. Instead, on both sides there was a not too latent undercurrent of suspicion and the impression that names and faces old and familiar were once again engaged in combat. As usual, growers are suspect because a continuing and convenient supply of cheap labor means life-blood to their business. Spokesmen for social agencies and the church are suspect because they are not engaged in agriculture and therefore cannot know what they are talking about; they are, at the best, professional do-gooders, theorists, academicians, philanthropists, or dreamers, and at the worst, troublemakers. Organized labor is suspect because it is organized labor and particularly because it has no concept of the farmer's problem, yet wants to get a foot in the agricultural door. Occasionally these suspicions erupted . . .

From a Texas congressmen: ". . . the processing of Mexican nationals has been administered in an unrealistic and unsatisfactory manner. I think that has been the consensus of the testimony of every responsible spokesman for the people who do the farming, who have to hire the workers, and who have to pay the taxes, and to stay in business. It is only those who indulge in theory and wishful thinking who disagree with that position."

From organized labor: "If the Congress wants to say that the importation of Mexican workers shall not be permitted if it has adverse effects on citizen workers, provided that this injunction is to be disregarded if the results would displease big farm employers, it should say so, plainly and directly."

From the National Farm Labor Users Committee: "Union officials don't reckon with the fact that fruit continues to ripen over the weekend and holidays. . . . When the farmer's whole yearly income depends on a few weeks of harvest, or even a few days, the callous attitude of American labor is intolerable and necessitates importation of labor."

From the Catholic Bishops of Wisconsin: "If once the influx of imported labor forces were greatly reduced or halted, then the citizen migrants would be in a position to bargain. . . . Obviously there are pressure groups which will strenuously oppose such actions. Since the pawn is a matter of human rights, and hence a moral issue, the Catholic Church cannot hesitate to stand for a position, however odious it may be to interested parties."

Assorted congressmen who were not members of the subcommittee gave opinions; those in favor of Public Law 78 had a slight edge in numbers over those against.

The bias of the subcommittee itself plainly leaned toward indefinite extension of Public Law 78, but, like the Texas congressman, it wanted some changes. These proposed changes became the nub of the controversy. The growers, it developed, wanted the law extended, but they did not like the way the Secretary of Labor was administering it; at the least they wanted it changed so that the Secretary of Agriculture would be brought into the process. Opponents conceded that immediate cutoff of Mexican labor would work a hardship on farmers, but they wanted a phasing off of the program toward complete termination on a fixed and not too distant date, and they did not share the grower view on administration. So sharp was this administrative issue that the first witness, Matt Trigg of the American Farm Bureau Federation, put it this way:

"This basic issue, in our opinion, is: Who is to write the laws of the country? . . . the Congress? . . . Or . . . executive officials . . . ?"

And Congressman Burr F. Harrison of Virginia phrased it more personally:

". . . the Secretary [of Labor] has had so many free hours, or such a superabundance of energy, as to find time to take the field in the so-called civil rights battle and to make a power grab for control over the harvesting of perishable crops in the United States."

Throughout the hearings contradictory statements were common.

Max Miller, introduced by Subcommittee Chairman Gathings of Arkansas as "a constituent, an outstanding agricultural leader in Arkansas, a farmer and a cotton ginner, and vice-president of the Arkansas Farm Bureau Federation," accused the Secretary of Labor of making Public Law 78 "a vehicle for administratively accomplishing certain things never intended nor visualized by Congress, and converting it into a Fair Labor Standards Act."

On the other hand, Congressman George McGovern of South Dakota, author of legislation supported by opponents of the importation, declared that in his estimation Public Law 78 "has now been transformed into a means of special advantage for a small number of large operators concentrated in a few states." The Commissioner of Labor of Oregon said that "by being overanxious to supply foreign labor to the nation's large farms, we have allowed a vampire bat to feast at the expense of our migrant and seasonal farm workers."

The Commissioner of Labor and Industry of the State of New Jersey offered his opinion from a different angle:

"The availability of almost a half-million Mexican agricultural workers in the Southwest at a typical rate of fifty cents an hour amounts to an unfair regional subsidy. Overproduction undoubtedly results when workers can be hired at substandard rates to work submarginal land. As a result, even in local markets, New Jersey's high-quality lettuce, tomatoes, and other row crops face unfair competition based on low wages and poor housing."

One grower betrayed his kind. Frederick S. Van Dyke, grower of beans, tomatoes, sugar beets, cucumbers, and grapes in California's San Joaquin Valley, spoke for himself and for the National Advisory Committee on Farm Labor. He declared that Public Law 78 was having a disastrous effect on the economy of the farming community; that it was depressing farm wages; ruining downtown merchants by sending farm wages back to Mexico; depressing farm prices by encouraging overproduction and so forcing the family farmer out of business; retarding technological development because when there is ample cheap labor there is no need for a machine; and straining the taxpayer by aggravating the social effects of extreme poverty. In short, Mr. Van Dyke claimed, Public Law 78 was hurting farmers, farm workers, businessmen, taxpayers—leaving not much of the public for it to benefit.

The pith of the contentions pro and con ran like this:

Public Law 78 was enacted in 1951 as a means of legalizing the use of Mexican farm labor.	Public Law 78 was enacted in 1951 at the time of the Korean conflict as a wartime emergency measure.
The Secretary of Labor has exceeded his authority, morally if not in the strict legal sense.	The Secretary of Labor has not exceeded his authority, which derives from the Wagner-Peyser Act of 1933.
Public Law 78 has not had an adverse effect on domestic labor.	Public Law 78 has had an adverse effect on domestic labor.
Public Law 78 has successfully halted the invasion of illegal aliens from Mexico.	Public Law 78 has successfully halted the invasion of illegal aliens from Mexico, but it has done so at the expense of domestic farm workers.

Public Law 78 fosters good relations with Mexico; the annual million dollars in earnings sent or carried in person back to Mexico represents an important factor in the Mexican economy.

If they were earned by domestic labor, the wages that now go back to Mexico would be spent in the United States to the benefit of the farming community; there are other ways to give economic assistance to Mexico.

It is the small farmer who would be hit hardest by termination of Public Law 78.

It is a few large corporation farms in five states that benefit from the use of Mexican nationals.

You can't get domestic labor to do the stoop work of agriculture.

Domestic labor would be available if growers had to compete on the open market for their labor; then they, like industrial employers, would have to offer wages and working conditions with some appeal to domestic workers.

In the midst of these contradictory assertions, each persuasively backed up with illustrations and data, the record was unequivocal on one point: during 1959, 437,643 Mexicans were admitted into the United States for temporary agricultural employment.

By any yardstick, close to half a million men make up a fair-sized work force. When did all this really begin? And why? In administering Public Law 78, what was the Secretary of Labor up to that so incurred the wrath of the embattled farmers? What was this legal Mexican invasion really doing to the jobs of domestic migrants? Was Public Law 78 being manipulated, as Max Miller declared, to raise farm labor standards? Or had it, as the Oregon Labor Commissioner protested, become a useful tool for large growers in a few states?

And incidentally, why were the five days of hearings in the

House Office Building confined to Mexicans? What about other foreign workers?

Of all these questions the last is most easily satisfied, simply by taking a look at the comparative size of the various groups imported. All told in 1959, 455,858 foreign workers were admitted into the country for contract to growers; of these the Mexicans accounted for 96 per cent. In the remaining 4 per cent, 5 from the Philippine Islands, 400 from Japan, even the 8600 from Canada and the 9210 from the British West Indies —all these were negligible in contrast to the nearly half a million Mexicans.

From reading the record the real issue comes clear like the handwriting on the wall. It is not, as Matt Trigg insisted, whether Congress or an executive official writes the laws; it is not whether the Secretary of Labor uses a broad or a legalistic interpretation of his authority; it is not whether Congress intended Public Law 78 to be a temporary wartime measure or a permanent means of curbing illegal immigration; it is not whether P.L. 78 did or did not adversely affect domestic farm labor; it is not even whether public funds should subsidize corporation farms with foreign labor. The heart of the real issue lies in the realm of industrial agriculture's progress toward adult and responsible membership in the American economy. Will organized agriculture, either voluntarily or by legislation, arrive at an adult and responsible attitude toward seasonal domestic labor? Or will it successfully bypass this step toward maturity and move directly into complete mechanization? There are signs pointing in both directions.

Speaking for the National Council of Churches, Rev. Shirley Greene added to his prepared statement at the hearings a comment that spoke of the ethics of the question: ". . . the testimony given at some of the farm hearings several years ago by representatives of growers of this type [large employers of migrant labor] was to the effect that 'We would rather starve than take price supports.' . . . I found myself asking, starve whom?"

Confronted with the moral argument that no profit is justified if it is made at the expense of exploited human beings, the power bloc in agriculture retreats to the incontestable position that farming is different; no other industry depends on such vagaries as frosts and drought and blight. The hard core of the corporate farm interests has not yet seriously listened to the argument that responsible labor relations might be good business.

Public Law 78 is one dramatic manifestation of this real issue, and the questions it raises deserve to be answered. Their roots are deep; they trace back to the California Constitutional Convention of 1849.

8. CHEAP AND DOCILE LABOR

Many people think that the importation of workers from a foreign land to do the stoop work in agriculture and the drudge tasks of industry is new. As a matter of fact, it is as old as history. The ancient Pharaohs imported farm labor, as did the Romans. . . . Our society encourages people to improve themselves—to have clean hands, comfortable working conditions, and the expenditure of a minimum of sweat. I cannot disagree with these premises because they are the American way of life.

—*Carl Fox, Artesia Alfalfa Growers Association, New Mexico.*

California came into the union as a free state, but not without a fight.

The year was 1849. In the midst of the gold-rush hysteria there were those in Congress and in California who saw a rich future for agriculture in the new territory. To realize this vision a cheap and docile labor force was crucial; this made a prime argument for slavery. Pro-slavery and anti-slavery factions contended with fury. Finally in September the California Constitutional Convention framed a free-state constitution and applied for admission to the union. A year later, almost to the day, Congress passed a bill admitting California as a free state.

The case for slavery was lost, but the opposition, as elsewhere, died hard. Until the Civil War the division between the Whig and the Democratic parties in California turned essentially on slavery. There was talk of dividing California into two states, north and south, free and slave, and there was even a scheme for a Pacific-coast republic.

Into the labor vacuum came the Chinese, welcomed by the gold speculators and the railroads as well as by farm interests. It was not long before American labor began to see a threat in Chinese willingness to work for substandard wages, and the white workers expelled the Chinese from the mines. Casual farm jobs remained open to them.

During the sixties and seventies the agricultural potential became a reality. Transcontinental railroads opened up eastern markets. Refrigerator cars expanded the market possibilities. Artificial irrigation made more land available for crops. Farms grew larger and labor needs skyrocketed, the bulk of them filled by Chinese.

By 1882 there were 375,000 Chinese in the United States, most of them in California. Stimulated by such groups as the American Workingmen's Party, Congress ended Chinese immigration by passage of the Chinese Exclusion Act.

The restrictive law did not apply to other Orientals, and the 1890s found Japanese working in logging camps and salmon fisheries and on truck farms. As their numbers increased, animosity quickened, and in 1907 the governments of Japan and the United States arrived at a "Gentlemen's Agreement"; Japan pledged herself to restrict emigration of laborers to the United States, and in return the United States undertook not to pass any prohibitive legislation.

Around the turn of the century Mexican peons began crossing the border for farm work. They went first to New Mexico and Arizona. A contemporary government survey of farm-labor wages in 1902 showing the differential between the cost of white and colored labor identifies the "colored" in Arizona and New Mexico as "Mexican and Indians," in California as "Japanese, Chinese, and Indians." In those days it was no trick to cross the border, and the new century was not far along before the pattern of the Mexican peon on farms of the Southwest, including California, was firmly set.

In 1917 a new immigration law threatened the Mexican tide, but the threat was momentary. Hardly had the law been enacted before it was waived to permit entry of Mexican workers for temporary employment in railroads, mines, and agriculture. Accordingly, between 1917 and 1921, some 23,000 Mexicans are recorded as legally admitted, and in the course of the twenties California more than trebled her Mexican population. In the same decade the whole country absorbed a million Mexicans.

The twenties saw also the beginnings of the co-operative employer organizations, progenitors of the line-up at the 1960 Washington hearings. The Valley Fruit Growers of San Joaquin County, established in 1921, became the first of these; and the Agricultural Labor Bureau of the San Joaquin Valley, organized in 1925, developed highly effective techniques of labor recruiting and wage fixing. Its sponsorship included six county farm bureaus, six county chambers of commerce, and the raisin, fresh-fruit, and cotton industries.

Thirty thousand Filipinos came into the state, too, between 1923 and 1930, but it was the Mexicans on whom the growers looked with greatest favor, especially in contrast to white labor:

"No labor that has ever come to the United States is more satisfactory under righteous treatment [than the Mexican]. He is the result of years of servitude, has always looked upon his employer as his patrón, and upon himself as part of the establishment," wrote the manager of the agricultural department of the Los Angeles Chamber of Commerce in 1929; and a lemon grower of Whittier wrote, contrasting his white and Mexican workers:

"Crabbing, grumbling, ill-natured complaining of conditions, loud-mouthed Bolshevistic propaganda, and other unpleasant behavior seriously interfered with the [Anglo] crew's activities. Several men quit before night, and the next morning only two or three out of fifteen reported for duty. . . . Mexicans as a rule work quietly and uncomplainingly and are well satisfied with wages and conditions. When a troublemaker appears, he is discharged at once."

The depression thirties brought to California the dust-bowl refugees from Oklahoma and Arkansas and provoked a reverse migration trend back to Mexico. From the whole country half a million Mexicans returned home.

As World War II drew domestic farm workers into defense industry and military service, grower demands for foreign labor became importunate. Most vocal were the powerful sugar-beet interests. As a result, in August 1942 the governments of the United States and Mexico signed an agreement providing for emergency importation of Mexican nationals for farm work. In late September the first supply of 1500 Mexican men arrived in California for contract to growers.

Beginning in 1943, similar agreements were negotiated with other governments. Small numbers came in from Newfoundland, British Honduras, and Barbados, and larger groups from Canada, Jamaica, and the Bahamas. Throughout the early forties Mexicans consistently made up about two thirds of the annual totals. The peak of Mexican imports came in 1944 with 62,000; this number takes on later significance when stacked up against the staggering totals for each year from 1955 to 1959.

It is a revealing commentary that Puerto Ricans were not included in the wartime emergency measure. They were readily available by the thousand; their "Operation Bootstrap" had not yet begun, and unemployment and poverty on the Island were considerably greater than they are today. Puerto Ricans did receive consideration in the early proposals, and there appears in the record only one explanation for their omission: the growers did not want them. There was, it appeared, a single strike against them: they were American citizens. The president of a Florida growers association explained this drawback to the Secretary of Agriculture:

"The vast difference between the Bahama Island labor and the domestic, including Puerto Rican, is that labor transported from the Bahama Islands can be diverted and sent home if it does not work, which cannot be done in the instance of labor from domestic United States or Puerto Rico."

In 1947 the Department of Agriculture, which had been administering the emergency farm-labor importation, announced plans to end its program.

Nevertheless, the importation did not cease.

What happened between 1947 and 1960?

In one sense the story is a saga, the saga of a giant effort of the governments of the United States and Mexico to bring order out of chaos by regularizing the use of Mexican labor in United States agriculture. The round figures on braceros imported and wetbacks apprehended give the skeleton outline of the tale; the glaring gaps between totals speak with eloquence and raise uneasy questions:

	Braceros Imported Under Contract	*Wetbacks Returned to Mexico*
1947	19,000	182,000
1948	35,000	179,000
1949	107,000	278,000
1950	67,000	458,000
1951	192,000	500,000

	Braceros Imported Under Contract	Wetbacks Returned to Mexico
1952	197,000	534,000
1953	201,000	875,000
1954	309,000	1,075,000
1955	398,000	242,000
1956	445,000	72,000
1957	436,000	44,000
1958	432,000	37,000
1959	437,000	30,000

Note how the bracero numbers fluctuate from 1947 to 1951.

Note the steady rise of wetback apprehensions to over a million in 1954 and their steady decline to a token 30,000 in 1959.

Note the total of 437,000 legal imports in the peacetime year of 1959 and contrast this with the wartime peak of only 62,000 in 1944.

Recall that 1959 closed a decade of spectacular technological advance in all fields; presumably the machine was busily taking over human jobs in agriculture—yet seven times as many Mexicans were imported to fill stoop-labor needs as were admitted fifteen years earlier in a year of labor shortage.

The story runs like this.

After the close of the wartime program Mexican nationals continued to be brought into the United States under contract through a series of international executive agreements. Responsibility for administration passed from the Department of Agriculture to the Department of Labor, a move that was to become a primary issue in the 1960 hearings. Complicated importation procedures involved the State Department, the Immigration and Naturalization Service, and the United States Employment Service.

These procedures made nobody happy.

Growers held that the State Department, bargaining in their behalf, allowed the Mexican Government to outsmart them. The contract, they insisted, gave all the protection to the workers and none to the employer.

As for the Mexican national, if he had a complaint that the employer was shortchanging him, the prescribed cumbersome routine of getting an appeal to the ear of the nearest Mexican consul or to one of the nine roving United States Employment Service inspectors (attempting to cover twenty-four states) demanded an ingenuity and a persistence quite beyond the resources of a non-English-speaking illiterate sugar-beet worker. It was far simpler for him to run out on his job.

Under the wartime emergency program Texas had no contract labor. The Mexican Government refused to supply its nationals to any state in which they would encounter discrimination, and on this ground Texas was excluded. As a result, hordes of Mexicans waded across the Rio Grande into Texas without formality and filled seasonal farm jobs at ten and twenty cents an hour. In the summer of 1947 the embarrassment of this accumulation of illegal aliens was removed when, by agreement between the two governments, the United States legalized 55,000 Mexicans illegally in Texas.

When the next peak cotton harvest season came around, October 1948, thousands of wetbacks evaded the border patrol and swarmed across the river around El Paso. The farm employers wanted them, and as a consequence the United States Government, instead of deporting them immediately, "paroled" them to growers. This wholesale expedient came to be known as "The El Paso Incident." It displeased the Mexican Government, and Mexico abrogated the International Agreement.

The next year another agreement was signed with a new twist: it validated the contracting of wetbacks who were already in the United States, and it gave them preference over workers from Mexico who had not violated the United States immigration laws. Consequently in 1949, of the 107,000 officially contracted Mexicans, fewer than one fifth were brought in from the interior of Mexico; the other four fifths were legalized wetbacks.

This invidious process put the United States immigration inspectors in an untenable position. Charged by law with the responsibility to deport illegal aliens, they found the government preventing them from doing their job.

To resolve the anomaly somebody worked out a musical-comedy technique. The immigration officer was allowed to deport the wetback. At the border an official gave the wetback an identification slip. With this in his pocket the wetback stepped across the boundary line into Mexico and became a new man eligible for legal importation under contract. The farce ostensibly saved the face of immigration personnel. It afforded gentle amusement to the Mexican peons.

One clause in the International Agreement made any grower employing wetbacks ineligible to contract for legal workers. Not unnaturally, this vexed the Texas grower. It irritated him to be policed by the border patrol; to see an agent riding horseback up and down his fields and know that the government was paying the rider twenty dollars a day to hunt wetbacks on the grower's property; to know that if the inspector found any, the grower's contracted braceros would be taken away from him. Obviously it was better business for the grower to hire nobody but the ubiquitous wetbacks than to bother with the red tape and expense of using the government channels, which might or might not be able to provide a specified number of workers on short notice. And so the number of legal imports in 1950 again shrank and the wetback tide continued to swell.

In August 1951 came Public Law 78.

It authorized the Secretary of Labor to recruit Mexican workers, operate reception centers, and supervise the process of contracting workers to employers. Because the Mexican Government complained that some employers were failing to pay agreed wages, the law provided that the United States Government should guarantee the wages stipulated in each contract. Further, it required a recruitment fee from each employer to cover transportation, food, shelter, and medical services for the national during the contracting process.

The law contained two provisions designed to prevent adverse effect on domestic workers. First, before nationals could be brought into an area the Secretary of Labor had to certify to a shortage of domestic labor; and second, the wages offered Mexican nationals had to be the prevailing wage in the area. Mexico specified that this wage be not below fifty cents an hour or its equivalent in piece-work rates.

The figures show that it took time for growers to shift from the wetbacks to legal imports. In the early fifties the wetback invasion became a nightmare for the Immigration Service. Seven hundred and fifty guards along a sixteen-hundred-mile border found themselves overwhelmed. On foot and horseback, by jeep and patrol car, roadblock and airplane they pursued the chase, quick to admit that for every wetback apprehended and dumped back across the border unknown numbers went undetected.

In 1953 the illegal invasion took on the proportions of a national scandal. Wetbacks turned up in the back rooms of Chicago hotels and holding Social Security cards in Pittsburgh steel mills. Attorney General Brownell paid a visit to the border, found the situation "serious and thoroughly unsatisfactory," conferred with growers, stopped off in Denver to discuss it with vacationing President Eisenhower. The following summer "Operation Wetback" went into effect. In July 1954 the new Commissioner of Immigration and Naturalization, Major General Joseph M. Swing, warned growers that the wetback roundup was soon to begin and that they should line up legal labor. The operation consisted of three parallel actions:

An enlarged border patrol, expertly deployed.

The enlistment of grower co-operation by means of the persuasive argument that bracero users need not fear competition from wetback employers because there would be no wetbacks to employ.

Streamlined recruiting processes to keep the growers supplied with braceros.

Organized growers generally went along with the program; small farmers deprived of wetbacks rushed to join grower associations. In a few spots there was tough opposition, as in the lower Rio Grande Valley, where the city of Brownsville is the capital of a three-thousand-square-mile agricultural empire with 300,000 inhabitants and an annual income of $300,000,000. Here the farm employers felt it a violation of their rights to be deprived of wetback labor. Newspaper headlines called the immigration inspection task force "an occupational army"; immigration officers had difficulty finding places to eat and sleep and buy gas; a drugstore in Harlingen displayed a sign: "Price double to Border Patrol till Cotton is Picked"; the *Brownsville Herald* published a picture of a crudely lettered sign that had appeared in the community reading: "Welcome Comrades of the Border Patrol, Soon We Will Rule the World." Responsible farm elements in the community ascribed all this to a small vociferous minority, but while it lasted it made life interesting for the Immigration Service.

Operation Wetback accomplished its purpose. Apprehensions slid from a million in 1954 to less than a quarter of a million in 1955 and on down to a low of 30,000 in 1959. Bracero contracts approached the half-million mark.

By the time of the 1960 hearings the wetback was history; it was the bracero who held the center of the stage.

Three events in 1959 drew fire from the grower bloc. On the surface only one of these concerned Mexican importation; actually the three are intimately related.

In February and again in September the Secretary of Labor came out in public in support of a minimum wage for agriculture.

In October four consultants appointed by the Secretary of Labor reviewed the eight-year operation of Public Law 78 and concluded that "as a practical judgment" it should be renewed on a temporary basis, but only with substantial amendment to prevent adverse effect on domestic labor.

In November the Secretary of Labor issued regulations providing in essence that an employer paying less than the prevailing farm wage or providing inadequate housing would not be entitled to use the United States Employment Service to recruit out-of-state workers.

These regulations stirred up such a storm of attack on the Secretary for exceeding his statutory authority that he asked the Attorney General for an opinion. This was duly issued in a formal ruling to the effect that the Wagner-Peyser Act of 1933 gave the Secretary the necessary authority.

Following this defeat, the Public Law 78 legislation supported by the growers of the 1960 hearings had two major provisions: it limited the authority of the Secretary of Labor, and it called for the Secretary of Agriculture to join the Secretary of Labor in making judgments on "shortage of domestic labor" and "prevailing wage."

A Washington rumor had it that the Secretary of Labor and the Secretary of Agriculture reached a compromise in the shadow of the White House. Secretary Mitchell agreed not to push at the moment for a minimum wage in agriculture; Secretary Benson agreed to oppose the legislation calling for joint administrative responsibility of Public Law 78 and to urge that the controversial regulations be tested through at least one crop season. Whether the rumor was fact or fiction, what happened was that each man acted as indicated.

In the Senate a subcommittee had held extensive hearings in 1959 and 1960 and on a variety of bills relating to migratory labor, but none had been held on Public Law 78 per se. Senator Holland of Florida sponsored an amendment to the wage-hour bill erasing the minimum working conditions specified by the Secretary of Labor for use of government-recruited interstate migrants. The amendment was defeated.

The 86th Congress did not decide the fate of Public Law 78. During the hectic closing hours of the post-convention session, on the plea of senior Senator Carl Hayden of Arizona that the expiration date ought to occur not in midseason but after the harvest was over, the Congress passed a six-month extension. With his plea went Senator Hayden's promise that no Senate-House conference would be held to prolong the extension beyond December 31, 1961, and that a thorough evaluation of the effects of Public Law 78 would take place early in 1961.

The stage was set for all-out war in the year to come.

Life on the Season

Prelude:

A GUIDE TO
FLORIDA CROPS
Issued by the Florida State Employment Service.

> It was worse now, for the topsoil had dried and blew up in choking brown clouds that sifted into eyes and ears and lungs, and burned with grains of silica sharp as glass. There was no shade . . . Some . . . chanted plaints that had no tune or author.
>
> > Born in a cornfield,
> > Raised like a slave,
> > Don't even have
> > The price of a grave.
> > —*Vinnie Williams in* The Fruit Tramp.

BEANS   "A hamper holds 32 pounds when full. The picker must have the judgment to pick the mature beans and leave the younger beans for later picking. He must exercise care in the handling of the bean plants, because damaged plants mean lesser earnings later on in the harvest.

"Crawling, crouching, stooping, walking, and kneeling are the physical demands of the bean picker. He works in the open and in the sun. The workday is from 7 to 8 hours, frequently delayed until nine to ten A.M. on account of dew.

"The wages are based on piecework and normally range from 50¢ to 65¢ per hamper. Therefore the earnings are contingent on the worker's willingness and ability to work. Some workers have picked as high as 24 hampers per day. A good worker should pick from 12 to 16 hampers per day. This, of course, depends on the weather and the yield."

TOMATOES "The picker must follow instructions as to picking of tomatoes ready for harvest, leaving the immature tomatoes for late picking. He must exercise care in the handling of vines to protect later harvests.

"Works in stooping position. Works in the open and in the sun. The workday is from 8 to 10 hours.

"Wages are based on both day and piece rate, depending on market conditions and location of harvest area. Piecework pay ranges from 8¢ to 10¢ per bucket. A good worker should pick from 80 to 100 buckets per day, depending on the weather and yield. Day rate ranges from $5.50 to $7.00."

POTATOES "The potato digger picks potatoes and places them in field crates or sacks. These crates hold approximately sixty pounds. The potato digger must exercise care not to leave potatoes in the rows.

"Works in kneeling position and progresses along the rows by crawling. Works in open and in the sun. Workday is from 8 to 10 hours.

"Wages are based on piecework and normally range from 5¢ to 7¢ per field crate. A good worker should pick from 75 to 150 field crates or sacks per day. Workers on potato harvesting machines earn 75¢ to $1.10 per hour."

CELERY "Celery is harvested by field machines, each machine requiring between 60 and 95 workers. The celery is cut by hand and placed on conveyor belts which carry it through washing vats for cleaning and then to packers who grade and pack it in crates. After being packed it is loaded on trucks for delivery to local packing houses for precooling, selling, and shipping.

"Celery cutters are required to do considerable crawling and kneeling on very damp soil. Work is in the open and in the sun. The workday is 8 to 10 hours. Others working on machine harvesting celery also work from 8 to 10 hours per day under damp conditions and must stand in one position for long periods of time.

"Wages for cutters are based on the row and usually average from $7.00 to $8.00 per day. Packers and others also average $7.00 to $8.00 per day."

9. THE FOURTH SUMMER:

The Grady Family

> If I could get me a steady job down in Virginia,
> I'd never go on the season. But a man's got to
> live.
> —*Robert Lee Hill, thirty-seven, in his fifteenth
> year on the season.*
>
> Being on the season gets you no place. On the
> season you are nobody.
> —*George Hill, fifteen-year-old migrant worker
> and nephew of Robert Lee Hill.*

That fourth year up the road turned into the scrappingest season the Gradys ever spent. Addie could feel her tongue lash out and she couldn't stop herself. It wasn't only with Henry; her tongue sharpened with the children too. It was queer how that awful aching love you could have for a person could show itself only in hateful words.

The heat made things no better. That summer Pennsylvania and New York in July felt hotter than any place Addie remembered in Georgia or Florida. It was the kind of heat that laid a great weight on your arms and legs and took away every bit of tucker you ever had. In every single camp they went to all seven of them slept and dressed and cooked and ate in one room; when it was ten foot by fourteen, it was a big room.

They had running arguments.

They argued over should they open the door and the window and fight the flies or should they shut the door and the window and fight the heat. Whichever way they decided, it didn't make any difference; they found themselves fighting heat and flies and each other all at once.

They argued over should they specialize in beans or should they pick at anything that came along. Henry wanted to specialize; being a specialist, he said, gave a man some dignity. Addie said who did he think he was? President Kennedy? All right, so if he was John Fitzgerald Kennedy he could specialize in being President of the United States, but if he was Henry Grady he just better crawl along after whatever crop he could find that could use him. Time was Addie could say something like that in a tone that made it three-quarters gentle spoofing and one-quarter serious; now when she said it the words sounded one-quarter serious and three-quarters plain mean. And all the time she was saying them she yearned to take him in her arms and comfort him, but she never did.

They argued should they let the kids work in the fields. Most of the parents had their children work. It sure did add up to more pay tickets when you did, and you couldn't say the extra money wasn't manna in the wilderness. Of course, some places you had to watch out for the inspector. There were special words you called out if you saw him coming, and everybody knew what the words meant; everybody, that is, but the inspector. Matthew thought this was a great joke, and he and Roosevelt set to figuring out a game. The children played it over and over again and taught it to the other kids every time they went to a different camp. The game went like this:

Roosevelt would shout, "Pickin' time," and all the children would drop to their knees on the ground and begin crawling along, making motions with their hands, pantomime-like, at picking beans, and they would singsong:

> *Pick* the ol' beans and *drop* 'em in the basket,
> *Pick* the ol' beans and *drop* 'em in the basket,

and all the while Roosevelt stood turning round and round with his hand shading his eyes, looking and looking at the edge of the sky, and then all of a sudden he'd yell, "Pick 'em clean, Joe," and every child would throw himself flat on the ground and bury his face in the dust. Then from nowhere would come Matthew limping along, dragging his poor clubfoot but managing to swagger and strut, and he and Roosevelt had a little conversation.

Matthew: "Hi, Mr. Row Boss."

Roosevelt: "Hi your own self, Mr. Inspector."

Matthew: "How's the beans, Mr. Row Boss?"

Roosevelt: "Not good, not bad, Mr. Inspector. Just about like they ought to be."

Matthew: "Any kids working here?"

Roosevelt: "Kids? What kids?" (Twisting his head in all directions.) "I don't see no kids. Do you?"

Matthew: "No, no kids. Thank you, Mr. Row Boss, sir, thank you, so long."

And Matthew would limp away; whereupon the little bean pickers would all jump up and race after him and tackle him, and down he would go in a heap of tangled arms and legs.

Sometimes the dialogue would get more elaborate. They would discuss the weather in detail, walk up and down examining the bean plants, stepping carefully over the prostrate children, and they would inquire after the health of each other's wives and children.

The first time Addie saw them play it she thought it was cute; times after that a notion nagged at her that it might not be just right for children to be playing at cheating the law. But what was right and wrong anyway? What was the law? Some

places there was a law and inspectors and children weren't supposed to work; or sometimes it seemed to be all right if they
worked until they were twelve or fourteen and then they had
to go to town and get working papers; other places it was all
legal no matter how young or old they were. If the law was
the law, why didn't it work one place the same as another?

Henry said children ought to work. It wasn't good to leave
them back in camp alone, and besides, it was a healthy thing
for kids to work, beans or onions or crops like that or picking
up potatoes after the machine. They couldn't begin too young,
and it was a sure thing they had to learn what it was like because they'd never have a chance to do anything else all their
lives long.

This was when Addie really sounded off. So they wouldn't
ever have a chance to do anything else, would they? Well, her
children weren't going to grow up to be nothing but stooping,
crawling bean pickers on the season. They were going to get educated, never you mind how; they were going to train for something good and real, something where you wore a necktie or a
uniform and used your head along with or maybe instead of your
hands and stood up straight behind a counter or carried a tray
or walked a beat or sat down in a chair with four legs in front
of a desk and wrote words plain and clear on a typewriting
machine. They were going to be somebody and they were going
to belong somewhere.

Right there to her astonishment and chagrin Addie found herself crying. Henry said, "Hey, there," and looked so stricken
that Addie said, still cross, "Oh, all right, so you're so crazy
about having them pick, let them pick, but only just so long as
there isn't any school around for them to go to. When we get to
a camp where regular school's going on in town and the bus
comes by, or where there's one of those summer schools for
migrant kids, then they're going to school, understand? No
more picking!"

One morning in July they hit a camp where they'd never been before. The truck left the highway, jolted down a rutty lane for a quarter of a mile, and ground to a stop. Cap Jackson lowered the tail gate and set up the ladder. Addie handed Princess Anne to Henry and took her turn climbing to the ground on awkward legs, stiff from riding a day and two nights in the back of the truck with no lay-down sleeping time.

Addie had a bone feeling about camps; either they were good or they were bad. There wasn't any in-between to a camp. What made it a bad one was partly a shiftless look, trash lying around and such, partly a smell, and partly a threat in the air.

This camp had a pretty name: "Willow Brook." Maybe that was a good omen. On the other hand, a name didn't have to mean a thing. She rubbed her knees and walked slowly around to get the feel of the place.

The hollow square where the truck stood was paved with dusty rubble. Three long wooden shacks, once, but not recently, whitewashed, bounded three sides of the square; the fourth side lay open to a beanfield. A patch of woods concealed the camp from the highway.

Each shack had a row of doors opening into the square. A scrawly number painted in black identified each door. All the threes were painted backward, and on each six and each nine the circle appeared on the wrong side of the stem as though children had been practicing writing in a looking glass. The doorsills were a good foot from the ground and there were no steps. To serve instead, some had cement blocks laid in front of them; a few had makeshift ramps of boards; three or four had inverted washtubs; some had nothing at all. Beside every door there was a window. There were no screens. Here and there stood trash cans spilling over with rubbish waiting to be hauled away. None of the cans had lids, and it all looked and smelled like the accumulation of several days.

There must be twenty doors in each shack, Addie decided. This meant twenty families times three, if the camp got full. More than half of the doors were padlocked now, and Cap's two truckloads of twenty-seven and twenty-three people, counting children, meant only ten more families. It would be nice if no more crews came in.

The scene was not without life, but it was a life infected with languor. In one doorway a brown-and-white mongrel dozed. In another two men played an indolent game of cards. In a third a small boy struggled with a piece of string to tie a roller skate on the bare foot of a still smaller girl.

The morning sun poured hotly down on a sprawling woodpile; on a clothesline hung with diapers and little girls' dresses; on a derelict washing machine; on four slender iron pipes, one in each corner of the square, each rising two feet high and each topped by a water faucet. In the middle of the square a rusty, old-fashioned iron cookstove rested on the ground against the wall of a shanty. The shanty had a stovepipe in the roof, advertising that there was at least one more stove inside. That wasn't all that was in there, either, because through the shanty's open door a voice out of a jukebox told the world, *I've got everything, I've got you.*

Nowhere to be seen was there a willow tree or a brook; the name was a fake. From a rakish wire incinerator a lazy wisp of smoke suggested a second source of the pervasive stench.

Addie made her reluctant judgment. This camp was a bad one. Could it be that she should have relented after all and agreed to their going up the road with Digger Burton?

Way back in the spring down in Florida they'd argued over which crew leader to join up with. Henry wanted to go with Digger. Two summers ago they had traveled with him, and he had really rooked them good; couldn't Henry remember that? How he'd promised them 75¢ a hamper for beans, and when the time came he said sure, he was paying 75¢ a hamper, but he had to take out 20¢ for his own share for getting them the job and 5¢ to pay on what they owed him for supplying food all the way up (that food was nothing but soda pop and crackers and sausage and cold baked beans out of a can) and for giving them credit at the camp store before the work began (six days it was, because of the steady rain, before the heat wave brought on the beans in a rush). And he charged them a dollar apiece when they crossed the James River ferry from Little Creek to Kiptopeke when everybody knew it was just 86¢ a person, and when they complained he said if you don't like it you know what you can do. And when they ended up the season with no money at all, he claimed they still owed him some (Addie was convinced they didn't but she had no proof) but they were such good people, he said, he'd just forget it. Rubbish!

This year he'd promised them a camp like a motel, with a real "rec" room and television and a cook truck that went right into the fields every noon with hot lunches. "And how much would he take out of our pay for all that?" asked Addie tartly. Henry persisted. Digger had got himself two buses this year to transport his crew; bus riding, said Henry, was sure a whole lot more comfortable than traveling in the back of a truck.

Digger owned an electric razor and he dressed flashy. He was a sweet talker and slick, and when Henry listened to him he forgot all about the crooked treatment of two years back. Henry was just like a child. The very sight of Digger put Addie's back up; as for Digger, he kept a wide berth from Addie. "He knows I see through him," she said to herself.

There were other reasons, too, why Addie didn't want the family to get tied up with Digger. He had a roving eye, and his eye had lit on Lottie. In the four years she'd been on the road with them Lottie had come to be a right pretty eighteen. She fitted nice into the family. Cap Jackson's boy Wilbur hung around her whenever he could, and she was kind enough to him, but she wouldn't have no truck with getting married. She meant to be a nurse, and you couldn't study to be a nurse if you were married to a bean picker, not even the crew leader's son. All the same, Addie could tell by the way Lottie tossed her head and gave a little secret smile whenever Digger's name was mentioned that she was flattered to be singled out for his favor.

Most of all, Digger wasn't in the least particular who joined his crew. He always had three or four roustabouts along who liked to pick just till they had cash to go on a real bender; he always had half a dozen women who were nothing but troublemakers and sluts, and he always had Satin Sadie, who didn't quite fit into the slut class because she wouldn't take up with just anybody. She was more or less Digger's girl, but she kept him guessing, and she surely did have a luscious look. Nights when she got in from beans, she'd dress herself up in purple satin and hang around the juke, and Henry admired her; she had such a cheerful way with her, he said she made a man feel good just to look at her. (Addie herself was plain and spare and she had no style.)

Cap Jackson and Digger were two different breeds of cat. Cap was big and homely and honest. He had two tumble-down trucks that he patched up from year to year; he drove one, and his wife Emma and his son Wilbur took turnabout driving the other. You lost a lot of time traveling with Cap because his brakes were always going bad or the oil leaked out or the signal lights didn't work and the road patrol would pick him up and make him post a bond and he'd have to telephone the grower long distance to wire him some money.

But Cap wouldn't take anybody in his crew he was a bit suspicious of; he had no use for the fast-buck boys and girls. Just let someone cause a ruckus in the truck or in the camp— Cap would fire him right out. Cap and Emma looked after their people if they got sick or in a fix, and Cap never took anything out of your pay, not even that social security that was supposed to take care of you when you were sixty-five. (Addie was thirty-one and Henry was thirty-three; who ever lived to be sixty-five or, for that matter, who wanted to?)

Cap was a preacher, too, and sometimes when they weren't working he'd put on a long-tailed coat and he'd preach a sermon so full of rousements he'd have everybody in the camp gathered round him on the ground a-swaying and shouting amens and brother-you-said-it-say-it-again.

No, they did right to stay away from Digger's outfit and stick with Cap.

The beans were running good, and soon there would be potatoes. The Gradys settled into the camp routine. Up at five, get the family stirring, send Roosevelt out to stand in line at the nearest spigot and fetch a bucket of water, heat up some wash water and last night's coffee, get the grits cooking. (A good thing they'd brought along that little old oilstove and didn't have to crowd into the cook shanty and fight for a spot on a wood-burning cookstove.) Lottie took charge of Princess Anne, bathed and dressed her and fixed her some powdered milk with a little coffee in it. Roosevelt and Sister spread up sandwiches for lunch, and somehow everybody got some breakfast down and turned up ready for the truck at six.

They worked for half a dozen different growers, and sometimes they had to ride forty, fifty, seventy-five miles to get to the fields. Then it was kneel and pick and pick and pick; change to a crouch and pick and pick; go back to kneeling and crawling; get your hamper full, collect your ticket and stuff it deep down good into your pocket, back again to pick, pick, pick. If you stopped to rest, you only felt hotter and stiffer when you started in again.

On the ride coming back the truck would stop at a roadside stand where they had a little store and the people would pour out and cash their bean tickets for cans and cold cuts and cookies. Addie liked to get potatoes and onions and canned tomatoes and pork butts and stew them all together in a kettle; sometimes it was neck bones and rice and black-eyed peas. Canned mackerel with cabbage and corn bread was good too. One night Addie would get dinner and Lottie would do the family wash, and the next night they would trade chores. Evenings there was nothing, just nothing to do but sit in the doorway or on the ground looking for a breath of air that wasn't there, till you got sleepy enough to fall on a straw-stuffed mattress and go out like a light, not caring was the window open or shut.

The heat hung on.

Came a day when a new crew moved in. A Wednesday it was, and of all the crews it might have been, whose should it be but Digger Burton's. Out of his two buses they spilled and they sprawled all over the lot, and they filled the air with their shrieks and their high-pitched talk.

How about that motel camp? Oh, that? Truth was (Satin Sadie told Henry and Henry told Addie) they went there, but they'd polished off so much red wine on the way that when the grower took a look and saw what shape they were in, he wouldn't have them on his place.

The chief difference Digger's crew made to Willow Brook Camp was they carried on loud all night so there was no more argument about the window and the door; you shut them both to help keep out the noise.

Henry took to sauntering over toward the juke every evening and visiting with Satin Sadie.

Digger was in his smoothest mood, meaning he oozed charm all over Lottie, and when he ran across Addie he became Mr. Courtesy himself.

Wilbur Jackson sulked.

Addie's temper shortened.

Come Saturday, massy white thunderheads hung in the sky

and it looked like a storm might break, but the heat only thickened. They picked late that night because nobody wanted to work on Sunday, and after they'd eaten, Addie was so tired she just told Lottie to let the kids play outside awhile and then round them up for bed, and she flung herself down and fell asleep, din or no din.

It wasn't till after sunrise that Addie rightly knew what went on that night, and then she got it from—of all people—Satin Sadie. Herself, all she could remember of the night was plain horror. Waking to a scream different from the regular noise, a yell with terror in it. Sounds of feet running and stumbling. Someone turning on the light and shaking her; that must have been Lottie. Then Henry, not walking but carried in flat out and feet first like a corpse, Wilbur holding his feet and Digger Burton his head. Henry's face a mass of bloody cuts, his eyes shut tight, his arms hanging limp, little moans coming out of his poor slashed mouth.

"It's a mercy he can moan, he's not dead." Somebody said this out loud, and maybe it was Addie herself. Digger handing her a bottle with a little whisky in it, saying, "Pour it on his cuts. It'll clean out the poison." Addie taking the whisky without a word and making short work of getting rid of Digger and sending Wilbur to wake up Cap. She and Lottie sponging up the blood and bathing the wounds with the whisky, and Henry really groaning now from the pain. Out of nowhere, Cap holding Henry's head with one hand and shaking white wonder powder out of a can over the cut places. Lottie ripping up her good white blouse for a bandage, and Henry opening his eyes and saying out of the good side of his mouth, "Addie, I'm sorry about this." Lottie trying to tell her what happened, and Addie just shutting her up. Princess Anne waking up and crying, and the other three children sleeping right through everything. After hours and hours, by some miracle they all went to sleep.

As she dropped off, Addie's last thought was, what a blessing the troopers didn't show up the way they do some Saturday nights.

Addie woke with the first ray of light, and she got up. In all the stir she'd hardly noticed the thunder and lightning and the rain; but now that she could think, she did recall it. As she stepped outside, the morning air had a light, cool feeling and a sparkle. Even the whole of Willow Brook Camp looked new-washed and clean, and it had a blessed quiet like a cemetery. As she took the bucket and walked to the spigot, who should be leaning out the nearest window right at her elbow but Satin Sadie.

"Addie," she called. Her voice was low for a change and it didn't break the hush. "Addie, how's Henry?"

"Hi, Sadie. He's all right. He's sleeping. Cut up kind of bad, but he'll do."

Satin Sadie's voice took on an earnest note. "Addie, do you know what happened last night? Do you?"

Addie looked down at her feet. "I reckon I know as much as I want to know."

"Not as much as you're going to know, Addie Grady, because I'm going to tell you exactly what happened and you're going to listen to me." Sadie hitched herself farther out the window. "That Digger got to making a big play for Lottie. Wilbur Jackson stood it for a spell, and then all quick like he whipped out his knife and went for Digger, and Henry, he put himself right in between them. That's how come Henry got his face cut up."

So that was it. Addie felt a great swelling pride inside herself. She looked up at Sadie and started to speak, but Sadie got in ahead.

"Now, then. That's not all you're going to hear. Do you know what Henry Grady talks to me about? By the hour? He talks about you. Nothing else in the world but you. The things

I know about you! How clean you keep your children, what a tasty cook you are, how you got a brain like a steel trap . . ."

"Satin Sadie, you're making this up." Addie tried to sound sniffy but she didn't quite manage it.

"I couldn't make it up. I'm not that smart. And that's not all. I know how, once you set your mind on something, not Pharaoh and all his army can't stop you. And I know how you're going to settle down for good some place and educate your children right out of this bean-picking rat race."

Addie was startled. "How does Henry know that?" she said, mostly to herself. "That about settling down. I never said that to anybody but Roosevelt, and he wouldn't tell. How does Henry know?"

"I don't know how he knows, but he does." Sadie chuckled, and then her voice grew secret-like. "Addie, it could be . . . it could be Henry knows more than you give him credit for."

"Could be he does," said Addie slowly. She leaned over to the spigot and drew her bucket brimful. She lifted it carefully, never spilling a drop, and then she set it down again and walked over close to the window. She put her two hands up on Sadie's shoulders and she gave her a kiss.

"It just could be he does," said Addie Grady.

10. A CLOUD OF WITNESSES

> And believe me, anybody who plunges into this
> problem has to have a strong arm and a sturdy
> back, because it is a maelstrom of emotion when
> you start asking questions about the migrant.
> —*John R. Fleming, Van Buren County Health
> Dept., Paw Paw, Michigan.*

Why did Willow Brook Camp have just four outdoor
faucets to serve sixty families for bathing, cooking, laundry, and
drinking? Why was there no hot water? No refrigeration? Why
was garbage allowed to accumulate in uncovered containers?
Why in all their travels did the Gradys never find a cabin with
a screen in the window?

Why was Cap Jackson permitted to transport twenty-seven
people in a truck for thirty-six hours with no stopovers for
sleeping? Why was he allowed to carry them in a vehicle that
was always breaking down? Why wasn't his license revoked?

Why was Digger Burton able to take out arbitrary amounts
from the Gradys' pay without giving an accounting?

Why didn't the growers for whom Cap and Digger provided
migrant workers deduct social security from their pay?

Why were Henry and Addie allowed to put nine-year-old

Roosevelt, seven-year-old Sister, and five-year-old Matthew to work in the fields?

Why are parents not paid enough for what they themselves do so that they don't feel the need of additional earnings from their children?

It is not an original answer to say that there ought to be a law, nor is the solution that simple. Nevertheless, legislation is one factor that should affect the lives of the Gradys and the Fontanezes; adequate legislation, that is, with provision for its enforcement.

As long ago as 1909 the problems of migrant farm labor were sufficiently acute to cause President Theodore Roosevelt's Country Life Commission to recommend remedial measures to Congress. It specified the need for good housing, for employment on an annual basis, for encouragement of thrift by the establishment of postal savings banks. Nothing happened.

In 1915 the United States Commission on Industrial Relations called for regularization of employment; bringing some order into the labor market; a feasible plan of providing transportation of workers; and sanitary workingmen's hotels with branch postal savings banks in connection with them. Still no federal measures were taken.

Through the years federal, state, and voluntary agencies have made repeated recommendations. Most frequently recurrent are those calling for coverage of agricultural workers under the Fair Labor Standards Act and the National Labor Relations Board; specifically for minimum wage, workmen's compensation, unemployment insurance, and child-labor regulation; registration of crew leaders and labor contractors; regulation and enforcement of housing, sanitation, and transportation standards.

Abuses and exploitation have not been eliminated, as the Gradys' experience shows. Nevertheless, there have been gains, some transitory, some whose effect takes time to be felt. Within the past twenty-five years six major attempts have been made within the government to attack the human problems of migrant labor.

1. *Utopian Experiment: 1936–1947*

In the middle 1930s the Farm Security Administration began the construction and operation of a series of model farm-labor camps. The common pattern provided rows of one-room wooden or metal shelters; central toilets, showers, and laundry; a clinic, a resident nurse, and visiting physicians; a child-care center; a school; a community house and outdoor recreational facilities. Most revolutionary was the philosophy on which the camps were managed: an elected camp council represented the migrant people in dealing with the camp manager and handling problems of order within the camp. These model camps were located in such widely separated areas of migrant-farm-labor concentration as California, Texas, Florida, and Suffolk County, Long Island. There were never enough of them to serve more than a fragment—certainly no more than a tenth—of the migrant population; but they did demonstrate what state, county, and local authorities and growers' associations might do, given the will, the imagination, and the resources.

The program survived grower opposition based on the fear that the democratic machinery within the camp opened the door to labor union organization, but it did not survive the postwar economy drive of the Eightieth Congress. In the late nineteen forties all the camps were liquidated or sold, to come under private auspices or local jurisdictions. In nearly all cases the housing and sanitation standards, the clinics, the schools and recreational facilities went out the window along with the concept of the self-governing camp council.

2. Prewar Recommendations: 1941

In 1941, under the chairmanship of Congressman John H. Tolan of California, "A Select Committee of the House of Representatives to Investigate the Interstate Migration of Destitute Citizens" held extensive hearings, and it made a series of cogent recommendations. These were sidetracked by Pearl Harbor.

3. Postwar Recommendations: 1946

In 1945 the Twelfth National Conference on Labor Legislation, representing forty-two states, the District of Columbia, and Puerto Rico, recommended "the organization of a Federal Interdepartmental Committee on Migrant Labor under the sponsorship of the United States Department of Labor . . . to study and report upon the working and living conditions of migrants, and pool the resources of the various agencies in order to devise and carry out a program to insure for migrants standards equal to those available to workers in other occupations."

The following May such a federal interagency committee was duly established under the authority of the War Mobilization and Reconversion Act. Its membership included representatives of the Departments of Labor and Agriculture, the Federal Security Agency, the National Housing Agency, and the Railroad Retirement Board. In addition to recommendations for legislation, for administrative steps, and for public action, its report contained suggested language for a labor-camp sanitation code; suggested standards for health services; a tabulation of state residence requirements.

As significant as any of the committee's findings was the interesting revelation that accurate information about migrant people was so difficult to obtain. A good many people had ideas, but nobody knew exactly who migrated or why; how much they earned or how many days they found work in a given year; how retarded were their children in school, what happened when illness or disaster struck them, or what they felt their own needs to be. Consequently the committee urged that funds be made available for federal and state agencies to work together to find out the facts: to assemble all possible information on the numbers and characteristics of the workers and their dependents, on their working and living conditions, on the trends in industry and agriculture affecting the need for migratory labor. It suggested such specific areas of research as patterns of migratory movement; duration of employment; annual incomes; housing, health, welfare, and community services; child labor, school attendance, educational achievement.

4. The President's Commission: 1950–1951

In 1950 President Truman created a Commission on Migratory Labor. This time the membership consisted not of government officials but of private citizens: Maurice T. Van Hecke, Professor of Law at the University of North Carolina as Chairman; Varden Fuller of the University of California as Executive Secretary; Noble Clark, Professor of Agriculture at the University of Wisconsin; William M. Leiserson, economist of Washington, D.C.; Archbishop Robert E. Lucey of San Antonio, Texas; Peter H. Odegard, Professor of Political Science at the University of California.

The commission held public hearings in Texas, Arizona, California, Oregon, Colorado, Tennessee, Michigan, New Jersey, and Florida. It heard testimony from growers and food processors; labor organizations; federal, state, and local government officials; social workers, health and educational specialists, church groups; and from labor contractors, crew leaders, and migrant workers. Members made field trips to observe actual

conditions and to talk directly with workers and employers on
their own ground.

In addition to making recommendations on housing, transportation, health, welfare, child labor, education, working conditions, and labor-management relations, the commission's report
emphasized the importance of more effective utilization of domestic workers and the elimination of dependence on foreign
labor. Administratively the commission considered the principle
of a special agency to serve the particular needs of migratory
farm workers—and decided against it:

"We do not believe that the answer to the neglected needs of
migratory farm workers is to create a new bureau or agency to
serve their particular requirements. The Commission is of the
opinion that in the long run the needs of migrants can best be
met by broadening and extending to them the basic services
which are designed to serve the population in general . . .
Something must be done, however, to achieve a more closely
integrated approach to the manifold problems of migratory
farm workers by these various agencies and to provide a voice
for the migrant where none now exists."

Though it seems a laborious, pedestrian, and bureaucratic
approach toward a solution of the human living problems faced
by the Gradys and the Fontanezes, it is probably true that the
most significant move made by the commission was its request
for a permanent interagency committee with staff and funds to
co-ordinate and stimulate extension of existing services to migrant farm workers. Further, the commission recommended
comparable agencies on the state level.

5. The President's Committee 1954

It was a five-member committee that President Eisenhower
appointed on August 26, 1954; it was a committee with cabinet
status. It consisted of the Secretary of Labor, Chairman; the

Secretaries of Agriculture, of Interior, and of Health, Education, and Welfare; and the Administrator of the Housing and Home Finance Agency. It was provided with an executive director and a working group from each of the five departments.

How many of the gains that have come about since 1954 can be attributed to the efforts of this committee and how many to the momentum already under way it is difficult to say; but it is a fact that concrete gains have come about since its formation.

In 1955 social security was extended to cover farm labor, including migrants.

In 1957 the Interstate Commerce Commission, on congressional mandate, issued federal regulations for transportation of farm workers more than seventy-five miles and across state lines in privately owned trucks and buses.

The Farm Placement Service's "Annual Worker Plan" for better utilization of domestic labor is getting its wrinkles ironed out and gaining in acceptance by growers, contractors and crew leaders, and individual migrants.

Twenty-eight states now have migratory labor committees on the federal pattern; these in turn have stimulated a variety of legislative measures on the state level.

Substantial research by government agencies, federal and state, has documented the characteristics, the travel patterns, the health and educational needs of migratory people and their families.

Programs in development include proposals to overcome the effects of restrictive residence laws; procedures for meeting the disaster and emergency needs of migrants; a guide to the responsibilities of workers living in camps; plans for financing the health services of migrants; the development of employment opportunities for migrants to the end of reducing the need to migrate.

6. *The Senate Subcommittee: 1959–1960*

In the summer of 1959 Chairman Lister Hill of the Senate Committee on Labor and Public Welfare appointed a subcommittee on migratory labor. Under the chairmanship of Senator Harrison A. Williams, Jr., of New Jersey, the subcommittee opened its Washington hearings with a statement of three fundamental propositions:

"A democratic and affluent society such as ours will not tolerate pockets of poverty and human degradation such as those presented by the migrant laborer.

"A democratic society deplores exploitation of the weak and uninformed.

"A democratic society does not accept the concept of inequality by birth; therefore, will not permit economic hardship, educational disadvantages, and health disabilities to be passed on from parent to child."

In subsequent months the subcommittee held hearings in Michigan, Wisconsin, Minnesota, New York, Pennsylvania, New Jersey, California, and Florida, and in the light of these it has developed legislative proposals in the areas of education, crew-leader regulation, minimum wage, child labor, and housing. They are sound proposals, and their enactment would be a giant step forward.

It is important to remember, however, that the process of reform is seldom rapid. Some of the most wounding aspects of agricultural migrancy—the stigma of stoop labor, community prejudice, the sense of belonging nowhere—cannot be legislated out of existence. The complexities of migratory labor, manifold enough in themselves, are inextricably tied in with the unresolved complexities of the total agricultural structure in the United States.

11. THE LAW AND THE PROPHETS

Behold, the wages of the laborers who mowed your fields, which you kept back by fraud, cry out; and the cries of the harvesters have reached the ears of the Lord of hosts.

—*James 5:4.*

Minimum-wage legislation does not cover the work done by Henry and Addie Grady and their children.

In the other major areas of difficulty reflected in the Grady experience—housing and sanitation, transportation, exploitation by crew leaders, social security, and child labor—there is a variety of existing legislation.

Why is it not accomplishing its purpose?

There are numerous reasons. Some of the laws are too general to mean very much. Many of them are not enforced. In some cases, as in transportation, the federal regulations need supplementary action by states. In other cases, as with crew-leader registration, a few states have requirements but these serve little purpose without federal control. Everything about the legislative picture is complicated because migrant life is complicated.

Here is the way existing legislation lines up.

Housing and Sanitation

In each of eighteen states there is some sort of housing regulation applying, at least in part, to migrant labor camps. Three other states—Arizona, Montana, and Wyoming—have codes affecting sanitary facilities only.

Neither Texas, with 96,000 domestic migrants, nor Michigan, with 47,000, has any regulation for housing or sanitation. Neither do twenty-five other states that use migrant workers. Those with no regulations, listed in order according to their number of domestic migrants, are:

Texas	Illinois	South Dakota
Michigan	North Dakota	Massachusetts
Kansas	Indiana	Mississippi
North Carolina	Georgia	Iowa
Missouri	Louisiana	West Virginia
Oklahoma	Nebraska	Tennessee
Virginia	Kentucky	Maine
Arkansas	Alabama	Vermont
Idaho	Utah	Rhode Island

Georgia, Indiana, and Virginia offer advice but do not regulate. Illinois and Rhode Island are working in the direction of regulation.

In the states where regulations do exist there are two jokers.

First, even with the most stringent codes, it is possible for a migrant camp to meet requirements and still be an inconvenient, crowded, and unsavory place to live. Picture an overpopulated third-rate motel with nobody responsible for keeping it cleaned up, and you get a rough idea, but only a rough one. Sometimes the requirements are so minimal that they help very little. The word "adequate" in a code is a convenient one to hide behind. Who is to say what is an "adequate" shelter or an "adequate" sanitary facility?

Second, there is the question of enforcement. To make housing and sanitation standards effective requires personnel and budget; a period of grower education; a system of certification; and something more than a token penalty for noncompliance. Minnesota, for example, has a code calling for a well-drained, comfortable, roomy camp site; floors of concrete or of smooth and close-laid wood (no cracks); screens; hot and cold water, and a toilet for every twelve persons. But Minnesota has one thousand migrant camps and *one*—and only one—sanitarian charged with camp inspection. It has no system for certifying camps. It has no penalty for noncompliance.

In 1956 the President's Committee circulated to the states a suggested code for regulation of agricultural labor camps. Its provisions did not differ substantially from those of the code proposed by the Federal Interagency Committee of 1947; it has had more influence than the earlier code, largely because the present committee, having a permanent staff, has been able to give it wide circulation. But it has a long way to go, and no state meets all the standards. The code calls for shelter structurally sound and providing protection against the elements; for no fewer than two rooms for each family of husband and wife and one or more children ten years and older; for a separate room provided and equipped for use as a kitchen; for wire fly-screening of all outside openings; for sanitization of mattresses between assignment to different employees; for one shower head for every eight persons, one washbasin for every twelve persons. It specifies that privies should be located no closer than fifty feet to sleeping quarters and no farther away than two hundred feet. Adjacent to each shelter there should be metal garbage cans with tight-fitting metal covers, and an adequate and convenient water supply meeting state standards for drinking, culinary, bathing, and laundry purposes.

There are factors on the farmer's side. The crop season is short, and he is reluctant to install expensive improvements and have them lie idle a good part of the year. Various plans have been proposed for low-cost, long-term loans contingent upon erection of housing conforming to the federal advisory code.

In general, it is those growers who collect rent from their workers who have the better housing, like Frank Pixley, in East Bethany, New York, who charges $3.00 a week per room. The state points with pride to his concrete-block units, the bottled gas for cooking, the hot showers, and the daily trash removal.

But also in New York State is a barrack in a permanent Negro slum outside Riverhead, Long Island, where a migrant crew of eleven adults and six children were found paying $50.00 a week plus utilities for five small bedrooms and a kitchen. There was electricity, a refrigerator, hot and cold showers (required by law), a gas stove, and an outdoor privy. "I got no complaint about the facilities," said Mrs. Robert Lee, wife of the crew leader, "but the rent do seem high."

There is the argument that migrants have no respect for property, that they are not accustomed to modern plumbing and don't know how to take care of it, that they would not use showers if they had them. It is certainly true of migrants, just as it is true of all people, that some are clean and some are dirty—except that for migrants keeping clean is harder. It is also true that if somebody is not accustomed to showers and plumbing it takes a degree of education to get used to using them. How anybody is to get used to them if he never has them is another question.

It is a paradox of our national mentality that the concept of housing and sanitation regulation in cities has become an accepted principle, yet similar regulation of migrant labor camps is resisted as an infringement of individual freedom. And freedom has strange interpretations.

"I did not fight in Korea," declared one southwestern grower, "to come home and have the government force me to put in shower baths for my cotton pickers."

Transportation

On June 7, 1957, at a Y intersection of Routes 301 and 102 nine miles north of Fayetteville, North Carolina, a flat-bed truck pulled into the path of a potato-laden tractor-trailer. In the truck rode forty-one Negro migrants en route from South to North to pick beans. Fifteen of them were injured; eighteen were killed, among them thirteen men, four women, and one six-months-old baby.

An ironic eleven days later the Interstate Commerce Commission issued regulations—on which it had been working for more than a year—covering interstate transportation of migrant farm workers. These specify seats fixed to the floor, half-hour meal stops every six hours, rest stops once between meal stops, and an eight-hour rest stop after each six hundred miles of travel; and they stipulate the type and condition of the vehicle. The Commission itself described the regulations as "tempered with an awareness of the unusual economic problem involved." Meaning what? That the passengers might be destitute? The crew leader quite possibly not too affluent? Or that the expense of too stringent requirements would up the cost of labor to the farmer? Probably it meant all three and with good reason.

In September 1959 the I.C.C. regulations were amended to authorize Commission representatives to order off the road all trucks and buses found to be in poor condition. The United States Department of Labor agreed that local employment service officers might assist migrants whom the new ruling left stranded.

But, as in the case of housing, even where law exists, enforcement is a serious problem. The Interstate Commerce Commission has insufficient staff to make the necessary inspections. Working together, the I.C.C. and the Labor Department tried an experiment. In the fall of 1958 they held a series of special meetings in Florida and Texas to explain the new rulings to crew leaders and "truckeros." These meetings were followed in the spring by a series of scheduled inspections in both states; few vehicles turned up for inspection. Apparently the crew leaders realized that their trucks and ancient buses would not pass inspection and that the necessary repairs would be expensive.

The I.C.C. provision for an eight-hour rest stop every six hundred miles poses practical problems. Migrant workers cannot afford motels, and if they could, discriminatory practices would keep them out. From the migrant's point of view, the bare outline of one ride with a caravan of trucks from Belle Glade, Florida, to a camp on the eastern shore of the Chesapeake gives some idea of how valuable an interstate system of rest stops would be. The account comes from a record of the trip made by a Florida Board of Health field worker who went along with the crew to get some data on migrant travel:

First Night	8:45 P.M.	Left Belle Glade.
	11:00 P.M.	Stopped at Fort Pierce for a meal but were told by the proprietor of the diner to move on.
	1:00 A.M.	Stopped in Melbourne for gas. Crew members were not allowed to use the toilets.
	1:55 A.M.	Made a bathroom stop in the woods.
Next Morning	6:20 A.M.	Bought cold meat, bread, and soft drinks at a country store outside Daytona Beach.

	12:00 Noon	Stopped for drinking water at a spring near Darien, Georgia. Water full of sulphur. . . . State troopers followed trucks through Richmond Hill; not permitted to stop.
Second Night	8:00 P.M.	Stopped in Bay Harbor, South Carolina, for meat, drinks, and so on at a country store. State troopers made crew stay with trucks during stop. One trooper stayed in store while purchases were being made.
	3:00 A.M.	One-and-one-half-hour stop for sleep. State troopers stayed nearby for entire time.
Second Day	7:45 A.M.	Took ferry. Police watched crew while waiting for boat. Not allowed to move outside ferry-house.
	11:00 P.M.	Arrived at camp.

For intrastate transportation just six states have specific laws governing movement of migrants in privately owned conveyances: California, Connecticut, New York, Oregon, Pennsylvania, and West Virginia. The President's Committee has drafted a code for state guidance, and it is curious that more states, if not concerned for migrant workers, are not concerned about the hazard to their own residents of unsafe vehicles on their highways.

Crew-Leader Registration

The crew-leader system grew up as a convenience to the
migrants themselves; it soon became a convenience to the
growers. Most crew leaders begin life as migrant workers; they
are the ones with a little extra drive and a little extra shrewdness.
Among Spanish Americans, the crew leader is often simply the
head of the family, and the family extends itself to draw in
distant relatives and friends.

In the West the more common term is labor contractor. Oregon has legislation that attempts to distinguish between crew
leader and labor contractor, requiring only registration of the
former but licensing of the latter. It defines the crew leader
as one who acts as spokesman for a crew. He may work along
with them in the fields; he may supervise them; he may transport them; but he receives no compensation from the workers.
In contrast, a labor contractor is one who provides a grower
with workers in return for an agreed remuneration or rate of
pay, or who furnishes board, lodging, or transportation for
workers for which he is paid by them. The same distinction
does not hold true in the East, where the term labor contractor
is rarely heard with reference to farm workers; there, the crew
leader customarily fills both roles.

For ingenious and unscrupulous crew leaders there is ample
opportunity to exploit workers and sometimes growers as well.
They have been known to recruit workers by misrepresenting
wages and working conditions; collect duplicate fees from
grower and workers for transportation; arrange for worker credit
at store or tavern on a percentage basis, or by an arrangement
whereby the proprietor ups his prices to the workers and he and
the crew leader split the profits. Crew leaders sometimes traffic
in liquor without a license, in marijuana, in prostitution; obtain
fees from migrants for health services rendered by county health
departments; bring crews into an area too early for the crop and

encourage them to run up grocery bills until they become desperate for work at any price; bring wetbacks into the country and exact special forms of payment from them on penalty of exposure to immigration authorities.

Contracting for seasonal farm workers has become big business. One operator is reputed to have main headquarters in the state of Washington and branch headquarters in Oregon, California, Idaho, and Texas; to own eighteen vehicles registered in Oregon, fourteen in Washington, six in California, and four in Texas; to have twenty-two crew leaders working for him; and to enjoy an estimated take of eight hundred dollars a day clear.

Regulation of the crew-leader operation is exceedingly difficult, partly because he seldom has a fixed place of business or residence. For him, being a migrant has its advantages. Eight states and Puerto Rico attempt to cope with the problem by some kind of registration or licensing, but the interstate character of the operation makes it highly impractical to handle it on a state-by-state basis. Federal legislation should be designed in such a way as to eliminate malpractices and to protect responsible crew leaders and labor contractors.

Social Security

Beginning in January 1955, farm workers were included legally under Old-Age and Survivors' Insurance. Where migrants are involved, making the system work proved to be exceedingly difficult.

From the outset growers resisted the idea. There was the bookkeeping, for one thing, but that wasn't all. In the words of one grower:

If you think I'm going to pay those niggers for working, and then pay social security to the government, too, you're crazy. In the first place, they don't want it—all they want is to be taken care of. In the second, the way they drink it up and gamble tickets for piecework, you don't know whether you're paying social security for the right ones or not. And in the third place, I'm not going to pay social security unless everybody else does, too, and most of them I know aren't paying, so the hell with the whole business.

So loud was the outcry that after six months the law was amended to make the crew leader function as the employer, unless grower and crew leader should sign a written agreement to the contrary. The grower rarely cares to sign such an agreement. The crew leader therefore becomes the man who must (for each worker to whom he pays $150 or more within a given year, or who works for him twenty or more days on a time and not on a piecework basis):

1. Keep a record of each worker covered by the law; his name, his social security number, and how much he is paid.

2. Make the appropriate deduction and give the worker a receipt at the end of the work period or the year.

3. Make tax reports, turn in the deductions, and pay the government the employer's share of the social security taxes.

For a crew leader, oftener than not a former migrant and almost certainly short on basic schooling, this is a tall order.

In advocating the amendment, farm groups pointed out that many migrants work longer for the crew leader with whom they travel than they do for one individual grower; consequently, when the crew leader functions as the employer, more workers stand a chance of qualifying for social security coverage than they would if the individual grower were considered their employer. But if the crew leader is too illiterate to keep the necessary records, or if he pockets the deductions, the migrant gains nothing.

Then there is the continuing problem of interpreting to migrants their rights and responsibilities under social security. They resent wage deductions for which they get only a promise of benefits in a dim future. It sounds like welfare, and what, they ask, has welfare ever done for them? In a vague way, too, they connect the deductions with income tax, and they want no part of that. Even finding a safe place to keep a social security card becomes a major difficulty for them. The Bureau has undertaken an extensive educational program, using specially prepared cartoon pamphlets, circulars in English and Spanish, posters, a film strip, and a film. Voluntary agencies working with migrants assist with distribution and interpretation of the materials.

The Bureau tells the story of Jack Reres, a Texas migrant worker who came in from the fields one evening in Arkansas, ate dinner in the camp with his wife and children, went to a tavern in town and was stabbed to death in a brawl. That night his widow called a staff member of the Migrant Ministry, an agency of the National Council of Churches; he in turn got in touch with the nearest social security office. Mr. Reres had a social security number, and he had been working all season. His family should have been eligible for benefits, but his record showed insufficient earnings. He was not a member of a crew; he had worked directly for several different growers in Michigan, in Arkansas, and in Texas. Mrs. Reres was able to give their names and locations, and the social security people went to work to investigate. Meantime the migrant workers in the Arkansas camp took up a collection to enable Mrs. Reres and her children to go back to Texas by bus. The investigation took months. It turned up the fact that Jack Reres did indeed have unreported earnings to his credit, and in time Mrs. Reres began receiving benefits.

Child Labor

During the fiscal year ending June 30, 1958, Labor Department personnel found, in an inspection of two thousand farms, well over four thousand children employed in violation of the law. Of these, more than half were between ten and thirteen years old. The violated laws are federal, and there are two of them.

The Fair Labor Standards Act, although not covering agriculture in other respects, does specify that children under sixteen may not be employed in farm work during hours when school is in session whenever the crop is to be marketed outside the state. One catch here is, as Pennsylvania Labor Commissioner Batt points out, that the grower may very well not decide whether to market his product in St. Louis or Boston or Pittsburgh until after it is picked and he gets his broker on the long-distance telephone and finds out the latest prevailing purchase prices.

Under the Sugar Act, if producers are to obtain maximum benefits, they may not employ children under fourteen—or permit those fourteen and fifteen to work longer than eight hours a day—in the cultivation or harvesting of sugar beets or sugar cane.

These are the only federal laws applying to child labor in agriculture.

Fourteen states have child-labor laws applying to work in agriculture during school hours; just eight of these laws apply also outside of school hours. In Louisiana children are not allowed to work more than a forty-four-hour week—except in agriculture. In Missouri the age is fourteen except for "occasional work with parental knowledge and consent"; the occasional work is often interpreted as picking cotton or tasseling hybrid-seed corn.

Growers have varying ideas about child labor. Some welcome regulations; they don't like to have children in the fields. Others say the children are better off in the fields than they are left to run wild in camp. One grower says he thinks it essential to allow children to work because otherwise the families will leave and find some place where they can all earn something. Another says he likes to have children as berrypickers because they are smaller and don't crush the berries.

Related to child labor are questions in the parents' minds about the value of school attendance; about the hazard of leaving children alone all day in camp; about the feeling that everybody must work to eke out the family income.

Equally relevant is the inescapable conclusion that comprehensive federal legislation affords the only effective protection for migrant children.

Earnings

There is one generalization that it is comparatively safe to make about migrants: their way of life is not geared to bank accounts. When they get paid in cash for their work there is always something to spend it for. Like more prosperous people, they are enamored of installment buying and layaway plans. If they feel the impulse to save, the sheer mechanics of getting to the bank when it's open are frustrating enough, and when you move every few weeks, it's easier to give up the whole idea.

The Labor Department figures that the average migrant works 119 days in a year and earns $710. If he happens to find some non-farm work to fill out the year, he may bring his take nearly —but not quite—up to $900.

Those who migrate within a single state earn less than the interstate migrants. Because they work fewer days and earn less per day, working wives earn just about half as much as their husbands. Total family earnings of Texas migrants average $1500 for those working only in Texas and about a thousand dollars more for those who cross state lines. (This is gross, without accounting for transportation expenses.) Earnings per day vary from crop to crop and from state to state. Texas carrot workers bring in $3.50 to $4.00 a day; for cotton, around $5.50. In other states workers out of Texas report a daily average of

$6.00 for Indiana tomatoes and $8.18 for the same crop in Illinois; $6.78 for beans in Minnesota; $7.28 for onions in Wisconsin; $8.44 for Washington peas; $8.70 for California vegetables. Highest earnings are found in the Pacific Northwest, the lowest in the southern states. Figured on an hourly basis, the range may run from 50¢ in the Rio Grande Valley to $1.25 in Washington. When there is a crew leader in the picture, the workers are usually employed on a piecework basis negotiated between the farmer and the crew leader.

The only federal legislation affecting farm wages is the Sugar Act, under which the Secretary of Agriculture determines the wage rate a grower must pay to be eligible for government subsidy. As for the states, Hawaii, Alaska, and Puerto Rico each has a minimum wage applicable to agriculture. Wisconsin has a minimum of 50¢ an hour for women and minors. *No other states have wage laws covering farm work.*

Inextricably tied in with the question of low pay when working is of course the irregularity of work. Both the Mexican national and the Puerto Rican contracts specify a minimum of work in a four-week period. Yet examples of written contracts of any kind with domestic workers are almost nonexistent. This is particularly interesting in view of one persistent thread that runs through grower testimony at state and congressional hearings and through many Farm Placement reports; namely, that it is virtually impossible to find domestic workers who are willing to do stoop labor. Suppose domestic laborers were offered a written contract with guaranteed hours of work at a specified wage on the same basis as—but no better than—that offered to Mexican nationals and Puerto Ricans? The idea is not revolutionary, yet it has been tried to any extent in only one state. For several years a few employers in eastern Washington have used contracts with domestic workers, but in the northwestern part of the state broccoli growers have long insisted that they

must have Mexican nationals. Two years ago the Farm Placement Service prevailed on them to try using a formal individual
worker contract, guaranteeing no fewer than sixty hours of
work every two weeks and earnings of not less than $1.00 an
hour. The result has been a successful broccoli harvest for two
consecutive years without the use of Mexican nationals.

It is true, of course, that industrial workers do not ordinarily
have guaranteed periods of employment; but they do have the
protection of a minimum wage and they do have unemployment
compensation. *Agriculture is specifically excluded from coverage
under unemployment compensation laws in every state except
Hawaii.*

Some argue that application of a federal minimum wage to
agriculture poses insuperable difficulties. How do you apply a
minimum wage to piecework? How about perquisites often
supplied free; housing, for example? At the request of Secretary
Mitchell, a detailed study of "Problems Involved in Applying a
Federal Minimum Wage to Agricultural Workers" was completed in April 1960. The conclusion of the study is that a
federal minimum wage in agriculture at an economically appropriate rate is both feasible and desirable; that the special
administrative problems would be difficult but not insuperable;
that such a program is a proper and useful part of public policy
looking toward internal economic development in the United
States.

Certainly agriculture has its own unique characteristics of
seasonal labor need and hazard of crop failure, yet why these
should justify exploitation of labor is not axiomatic. Still less
easy is it to dispel the idea that an industry heavily subsidized
with federal funds ought not to be permitted to operate without
reasonable guarantee of a living wage to its workers. This is the
philosophy inherent in the Sugar Act; it needs to be carried
over into high-level considerations of the total agricultural pic-

ture in the United States. Otherwise the bitter conclusion is inescapable: migrant workers who are United States citizens can't hope to do as well as others represented by the government of Mexico.

Interlude: DAY HAUL

> . . . if you demand on the one hand
> the raw material of poetry in
> all its rawness and
> that which is on the other hand
> genuine, you are interested in poetry.
> —*Marianne Moore.*

The afternoon was nearing its end when Marianne Moore (*not* the poet) asked her question.

All morning she just sat and listened, up there on the eighteenth floor of the Commonwealth of Pennsylvania Building at Broad Street and Spring Garden, she and her two companions. One thing struck Marianne about that morning discussion, and it troubled her. After lunch all three of them testified. And then Marianne spoke what was on her mind.

Marianne Moore, Rufus Boone, and Grant Madison had been invited to appear before the Senate Subcommittee on Migratory Labor as authorities on the day-haul operation.

For the past year Mrs. Moore has owned and operated "The Farmers' Inn" at 26 South Street in Philadelphia; during the three preceding years she, like Rufus and Grant, was a day-haul crew leader, rounding up hands before daylight, transporting them to farms in Pennsylvania and New Jersey, and returning them each evening. Now Marianne runs her restaurant and works for Rufus Boone as a helper.

During the morning Marianne and Grant and Rufus listened in silence as labor leaders, spokesmen for church and social agencies, and state officials talked about housing, sanitation, a minimum wage for agriculture, crew-leader registration, migrant education, child labor, and health. The entire morning discussion centered not on the day haul but on the interstate migrant worker.

At lunch time the chairman concluded the session on a bright note: "We saw an example of . . . local acceptance and a lot of other good things out in Michigan, where the daughter of a migrant farm family became 'Miss Michigan' in the Miss America pageant in 1953, which was proof of many things, we thought." Whereupon, at 1:05 P.M., the subcommittee recessed.

At 2:15 they reconvened. Mrs. Moore and her companions had no prepared statements, and their testimony became an informal question-and-answer period.

Grant Madison, as he told the subcommittee, has been a day-haul crew leader in Philadelphia for nine years; he has three buses. Rufus Boone's experience goes back to 1930, and he now has three buses and four trucks. Thirty-five to forty miles is about the limit of an efficient day haul. Sometimes they go to farms in Pennsylvania; sometimes they cross the Delaware River into New Jersey. They begin in the spring, about the middle of April, with spinach, then on through strawberries, blueberries, and tomatoes, back to weeding and cutting spinach, getting up parsley and parsnips, and so on into November.

Chairman: "Of course, machinery is creeping into the picking operation, isn't it?"

Mr. Madison: "Yes. I know one place I do a lot of work at and they have machines that cut the spinach and all, but still they have to use a lot of help—they have got the machines to help on the spinach, but when they carry it in and run it over the belt, they have to get people to pick the weeds out."

Chairman: "They have got a bean picker." The chairman

was referring to the new mechanical bean picker, which takes just two people to man it. It clears the field in one operation. In hand harvesting most growers use a crew three times on the same field to get the later ripening beans. This was a tender point with Grant Madison.

Mr. Madison: "You can only go over it one time, and that takes it."

Mr. Madison transports seventy-five or eighty people every morning; Mr. Boone, with his fleet of both buses and trucks, carries, in the peak of the season, somewhere around 300. The crew leaders use no advertising techniques to get their people; the word just spreads around. The crew leaders tell the people what they are going to pick and what the pay will be, and the people choose which crew they will go with.

Later in the hearings it came out that there are more than a hundred crew leaders in Philadelphia and that a similar operation goes on over in Camden. A government official reported that between two and three thousand workers are hauled out of Philadelphia every morning. Both men and women go, but "I don't take no kids," said Mr. Madison. "Eighteen or nineteen or twenty years on up."

As a helper to Rufus Boone, "I am a food lady," Marianne Moore explained. "I have to do that. I serve the food. And of course my sandwiches are twenty-five, thirty, thirty-five. Part I feed before they ever go to work, because they are hungry. I have a restaurant at 13th and South where they load the buses out. . . . They gather on the corner at four and four-thirty. . . . I go down there at four o'clock; I open my place of business at four. . . . We were loading on the corner of 13th and South for years, right on the corner. In the morning from four o'clock, say around five o'clock, it looked like a New Year's parade there with the farm people. Well, they had a lot of excitement, but it was not the farm people at all. The neighborhood got together and they signed a petition, you know, and they had us chased away from down there to 9th and Rodman, 9th and Nordane, somewhere down there. . . . We didn't stay there but three days. Then they chased us over to Bainbridge Street, from Broad to 13th. We have our neighborhood there; that is where we load at now. On both sides of the street from Broad Street to 13th is loaded with buses. . . . On Tuesday you can't hardly get nobody . . . The first thing you say, 'Come on, get on the bus and go with me.' 'Oh, I can't go today. I have got to stay in today and sign my check—today's my check.' . . . I imagine they mean the relief check or whatever they get. I don't know— I don't even ask them. But whatever kind of check they have got to get they have got to sign for; mostly it comes on a Tuesday . . . North Philadelphia is on a Thursday, but downtown is on a Tuesday. So we go down to the farmer with a bus half loaded with people, and the farmer wants to know, 'Where are all the people, Marianne? Where is the people?' And I say, 'What can I do, Rocky, I brought all I could get.' So . . . we have to take our buses from South Philadelphia and go up to North Philadelphia and finish loading the bus, which I have done plenty of times."

The chairman asked about terms of employment. "I gather you have contracts at the other end with more than one grower . . . could you give us an idea of the nature of that contract?"

"Well, the only contract that I ever gave," Grant Madison spoke up, "was just the word of mouth. Everybody that I ever promised, I always filled it . . . I go and see him, or sometimes he calls me and tells me to come out, he wants to talk with me, and he tells me what he has got to do, and then he tells me what he is going to pay . . ."

Chairman: "I see. He will tell you he has got a crop and how long he will need you, and how many people . . . What financial agreements do you make?"

Mr. Madison: "He tells me—if he is going to pick tomatoes, he tells me what he will pay; he will pay about fourteen cents . . . a basket . . . a bushel basket . . . And the people get eleven cents and I get three cents . . . He knows exactly what I am paying them. . . . What would help a lot would be if they had a standard piecework price, because the people don't make much picking tomatoes and blueberries and strawberries because the price is so low, and there is nothing you can do about it. . . . Well, 75 cents an hour, a lot of them pays that, and if you want to set that price, of course, that would be all right, but . . . If you set a minimum price on piecework in our work, that would be the real thing."

Mr. Boone: "The pieceworkers work a whole lot faster to try to make something. They have got to work faster."

Mr. Madison: "I have had people out picking cucumbers by the hour, and I would have maybe fifty or sixty, and some would be going to get water, and some telling all kinds of funny things, and this and that, and some wouldn't pick only seven or eight baskets of cucumbers. . . . And I told the farmer, 'You are killing yourself. You ought to get on piecework.' . . . And if a guy working by the hour didn't get but four or five (baskets), he will want to get paid for all day . . . the man that speeds his work up maybe doesn't do it too good, and that hurts, too, but he has got to do that, maybe, to make six or eight dollars."

The average day's take for a normal picker, he said, would be four or five dollars. There is no charge for transportation. Most crew leaders carry food and sell it during the day.

Chairman: "We have heard about bread being sold at fifty cents a loaf." According to the record, at that point Mrs. Moore gasped. Plainly, as a food lady, she was horrified at such exploitation.

Mr. Madison: "All kind of things happen on some of those jobs."

The chairman was interested in the behavior of the crews "We have heard a lot of complaints," he said, "that farm workers that go out on the crops don't behave very well and they waste their money and aren't too responsible. Do you have any comments on that?"

Mr. Madison: "Well, there are crew leaders—there are some crew leaders, you know, that sell people wine and stuff like that. And that is where that comes in at. . . . If the farmer can get a good day's work out of my people, he wants me to come out the next day, but if I go out there and all of them get drunk, why he don't want me back. . . . When you go to a farm and he has got seven or eight different contractors, he has got me and somebody from over there all huddled up together, different contractors on this one farm, that is when the drinking comes off, because somebody is in a gang that has got a car and is selling food or drinks—I don't have any control over that."

Mr. Boone: "Most of the crews have their own ruling. We don't allow so-and-so on this bus and so on. But if the other fellow does, that is his business."

Mr. Madison: "You see, some farmers, at times they have maybe eighteen or twenty crew leaders there . . . that is when a lot of things go on."

Both Rufus and Grant agreed that federal registration of crew leaders would be a good thing.

"A fellow took away a gang this year," said Grant, "and he collected the money and he walked away and left the people in the bus."

Already in Pennsylvania crew leaders are required to register. "It means a lot to us, too," Mr. Boone declared, "because those fly-by-nights come in and get the cream and we get the worries, and by we helping out on this, I think it would be a good thing."

The chairman spoke to the three of them with appreciation for their help and for their spending the whole day with the committee.

"I don't mind a bit in the world," said Grant Madison. "Are you going to do anything about the piecework?"

The chairman agreed to tell Senator Clark "what you want and want fast."

Then it was that Marianne Moore brought out what had been worrying her, nagging at her ever since the morning testimony about the living conditions of interstate migrants.

"Senator," she said, "may I ask this one question? On these camps where these people are mostly from out of different states, what are they supposed to do when they get sick? Is there some way you can give them a nurse or a doctor once a month?"

Chairman: "You are talking about the people that have migrated? Not your people?"

Mrs. Moore: "But I just wanted to ask that question. I notice this morning it wasn't mentioned. Is there any way you can get a doctor for those people that are in the camps?"

The chairman did his best.

"We have seen a lot of trouble, a lot of problems in this area. Some crew leaders are very responsible. When anybody gets sick, the crew leaders will take them immediately to the most available doctor or hospital. Others are negligent, and in some places there is no medical care readily available. Really it is one of the serious problems. And we hope this is one area where our committee can propose some legislation or perhaps other ideas that will make medical care available to the farm worker. I agree with you that it is a serious problem. I am glad you mentioned it.

"Thank you."

12. BORN IN ASPARAGUS:

The Fontanez Family

> . . . sorrow nor sweating nor aching back, sick-
> ness, nor pity, hope gone, heaven's deafness;
> . . . not thunder nor the rustling worms nor
> scalding kettle nor weeping child shall rouse us
> where we rest.
>
> —*James Agee.*

Miguel Fontanez, the child of Juan and Dolores, was born
in St. Albans United States Naval Hospital in Queens.

It was different with the uncles and aunts of Miguel. They,
like his father, were the children of Pablo and Annunciata
Fontanez, and they were born on the season. Miguel's uncle
Pedro, now seventeen, was born in onions; his aunt Elena, now
fifteen, in cotton; his aunt Ramona, now ten, in tomatoes. Not
actually in the fields, to be sure, except in the most dire
emergency; it was simply that this was their way of remember-
ing. The crop was the Fontanez family calendar, and it was
the crop that marked the large events of their lives. Between
Elena and Ramona there had been twin girls, Lola and Lolita;
they were born, they lived five days, and they died, in carrots.
All these births took place while the family was still migrating
within the state of Texas and before the swarms of wetbacks

started them traveling each spring across state lines looking for work. After Ramona, Arturo arrived in Arkansas cotton, lived through a year of interstate migration, and back again in Arkansas cotton, on his first birthday, he died.

As a matter of course Felicia Fontanez, the grandmother, a *partera* of note in her native Mexican village and also in Crescent City, Texas, delivered all the children. The Fontanez family took it for granted that Felicia would do the same for Dolores' second baby. Even to Juan himself this was natural, inevitable, and right. Miguel was born in a hospital, not because it was the preferred procedure, but because St. Albans was the best substitute the United States Navy could offer for Felicia.

Dolores had a different idea.

As the family picked the last of Mr. Van Leyden's strawberries and trucked on to snap asparagus in Illinois, the circumstance of Miguel's birth in a hospital took on epic significance.

It was a year ago in the spring that Juan finished his three years in the Navy and came back to Crescent City, Texas, bringing with him his Puerto Rican wife, Dolores, and their son Miguel, then three months old.

The Fontanezes were enraptured with Miguel.

With the single exception of Pablo they gave to Dolores a more temperate reception. Pablo was inordinately proud of his daughter-in-law; indeed, he was exuberant. Manuel accepted her with cordial ceremony, but at a distance. Felicia regarded her with outright suspicion, making it evident that she drew a line between one who was Spanish by way of Mexico and one who suffered the humiliation of birth in Puerto Rico. This did not disturb Dolores. She was fascinated by the dainty old lady with the straight spine and the inflexible Mexican code; by her strong, gentle fingers with the sure and healing touch; by her insistence that the juice from an onion fried in olive oil and sweetened with honey would relieve Pedro's asthma; by the fact that with this treatment the asthma did indeed subside.

Dolores was troubled, though, that Annunciata did not like her. She longed to love Juan's mother and to be loved by her. Yet, try as she would, Dolores could not please her. To Annunciata, Juan, her eldest, represented perfection. No girl could be good enough for him and certainly not this one from Puerto Rico with her talk, talk, talk of St. Albans United States Naval Hospital.

It was ten years since Dolores and her family flew from San Juan to New York to make a new life. They made it in a tenement, in the Williamsburg section of Brooklyn. Two years later, when Dolores was twelve, the tenement burned and the family with it, all but Dolores herself. Neighbors took her in, and she lived with them and continued going to school. She did well in high school, and on graduation she found work as a temporary clerk at the United States Naval Base in Brooklyn. There she met Juan, on duty at the Navy Yard dispensary.

Dolores did not have conventional good looks, but she had grace; she had a dignity that masked her native diffidence; and for Juan she had stars in her eyes. Juan told her about his family and their travels up and down the United States; about the house in Crescent City, Texas, to which they came back always in time for the Christmas fiesta; about his own private ambition to become a big labor contractor with a fleet of trucks. Within a week they were married.

In spite of her admiration for Felicia, Dolores wanted her second baby born in a hospital. She still had a hundred dollars carefully treasured from her Navy Yard job; this she would use to pay the bill. She did not worry about finding a hospital when the time came. It would not be so fine as St. Albans but this was a detail. Her real problem was more immediate: when and how to break to the family the news of her intention.

In Illinois asparagus there came a family crisis. Elena violated the family code. She slipped out one night and went to a dance hall in town with a migrant boy. Dolores took Elena's part, and this time she felt the stigma of disapproval from all the adult members of the family, including her husband and even Pablo.

Assuredly this was not the moment to tell them all that she meant to have her baby in a hospital, but before she knew it, out it came. For weeks she had been thinking and thinking how to say it without hurting Felicia, and now she had done it in the worst possible way in front of them all, at the worst possible time when they were all keyed up and angry. She was heartsick. But she did not change her mind, not even when it came out that Felicia and Manuel had come on the season—deciding this just two days before the truck left Crescent City—only so that Felicia might preside at the birth of Juan's second child.

The camp where they were living just outside Plain City, Illinois, was a large one, owned and operated by the canning company. Two evenings a week a doctor from town came out to hold a clinic at the camp. It was his own idea; the company made a room available. Dolores went to see him.

Dr. Schwartz was an Austrian-Jewish refugee. The circumstances that had landed him practicing medicine in an Illinois community of 15,000, ninety-nine miles south of Chicago, had given him more than ordinary insight into what may happen when conflicting culture values collide. In three years of service for the canning company he had acquired a fair command of the Spanish language and he had become sensitive to some of the things that are important to Mexican American families.

He drew Dolores' story from her, all of it, beginning with the flight from San Juan and straight on through the tenement fire, the kind neighbors, her high-school teachers, her work at the Navy Yard, her marriage, St. Albans Hospital, her reception by the family in Crescent City, and on to the scene over Elena's escapade. Dolores sketched a picture for him of Felicia, her birdlike head, her strength, her iron will, her skillful fingers, and her folk remedies that worked.

Dr. Schwartz thought for several minutes. Then he said:

"Mrs. Fontanez, I will go to see your family. Not tonight—too many people are waiting outside to see me. But I will talk with your family. Do not tell them I am coming. And do not worry. We will work this out."

Dolores' misery eased a little, but she still did not see the solution. The doctor's impromptu visit to the family was a great success. He apologized for his Spanish, which was heavily flavored with gutturals, and the Fontanezes assured him it was excellent. He ate three *tortillas* and complimented Annunciata on her cooking. He admired Miguel. He conversed with Elena and Ramona as though they were grown up. He joked with Felicia about their being in the same business. He agreed to come out the next evening and eat with them and to bring a baseball bat and play a ball game with Juan and Pablo and Pedro.

On his third visit he addressed himself mainly to Felicia. They talked a long time, and as he left he arranged to call for her the next evening and take her into the hospital to see the delivery room and the maternity ward. She wanted him to take Manuel also, but Dr. Schwartz said no, this was a professional expedition.

Two weeks later Miguel's sister was born. The event took place in the Plain City Community Hospital. The baby weighed five pounds, eight ounces. Her parents named her Felicita Schwartz Fontanez.

13. STAYING ALIVE

E.C.: Twelve-month-old Mexican American
male admitted Palo Alto-Stanford Hospital July
20, 1960. Chief complaint: 8 days vomiting and
diarrhea. Immunizations: none. Thin, moderately dehydrated child with sunken eyes, poor
turgor of the skin, lethargy, and deep breathing.
Neck supple. Diagnosis: iron deficiency anemia;
pneumococcal meningitis; diarrhea due to patho-
genic E. coli (group A-#055).
—*Case cited in report of public health task force
led by Dr. R. Bruce Jessup of the Department
of Pediatrics, Stanford School of Medicine. July–
October 1960.*

Six weeks before his admission to the hospital, E.C., his
seven brothers and sisters, and his parents came from the San
Joaquin Valley north to Mountain View and moved into a tent
camp set in an apricot orchard. Their tent provided the family
with one room, nine by twelve; a dirt floor strewn with garbage
and refuse; two beds in which slept the family of ten; two
stoves (one butane, one kerosene); no window; and a heavy
population of flies. E.C.'s mother, aged thirty-three, was thirty-
three weeks pregnant with her ninth child.

Barely visible from the road, the camp consisted of E.C.'s
tent and three others; one substandard building (locked); one

substandard trailer; one dwelling made of wooden fruit trays; three water spigots; one wooden privy, full and nailed shut but open to flies; and three chemical toilets for the eighty residents.

The state of California has housing and sanitary regulations applicable to migrant-farm-labor camps, with a penalty for violations (maximum $200.00). When the medical task force discovered E.C., the camp at Mountain View had been operating for two months without the knowledge of the health department.

E.C. is an extreme but by no means an isolated case, either in California or in any other state in which migrants live and work.

It is an odd fact that professional persons—teachers, welfare workers, ministers, police—who come into direct contact with migrants occasionally remark that migrant health is not so bad as they would expect it to be among people of such precarious income and hazardous living conditions. For these comments public-health personnel offer several explanations. Migrant people do not habitually think of themselves as sick; as long as they can get around they get along. The ones who are too sick to get around don't migrate. There is the strong probability that the children develop a natural immunity to germs. One reason is statistical and grim: there is in migrant camps a high incidence of infant mortality; only the tough survive.

In medical reports on migrant health two interesting observations recur.

First, mental illness is not prominent among migrant people. Certainly their crowded living invites emotional disturbance. There has been no research in this area, but an explanation does suggest itself: the conventional middle-class pressures on children to conform and to excel are infrequent in migrant parents; and related to this is a passive, fatalistic tendency of many of the parents to accept life as they find it.

Second, migrant mothers regard conditions like children's chronic head colds, skin eruptions, and infant diarrhea as normal. Babies are always this way; of course children's noses run; certainly their skin is broken out and blotchy. You don't fret, you just cope the best you can, because children are like this.

Prevalent ills among migrants are the ills that affect the rest of the population; only in degree are they occupational. Heading the list are dental defects; abnormalities of one kind or another are found in the teeth of three quarters of the children and 95 to 100 per cent of the adults: pyorrhea, abscesses, caries, erosion to the gum line. There is the inevitable impetigo and a variety of other skin troubles, including a kind known in the north as "Florida sores." There is a nutritional type of anemia; scurvy; pellagra; rickets; febrile tonsillitis; copious nasal discharge; asthma; intestinal parasites; dysentery; diarrhea, both infant and in epidemics involving the whole family, causing dehydration and sometimes, especially among the younger children, death; inflammation of lymphatic glands; orthopedic defects; congenital heart conditions; vision and hearing defects. Among adult migrants who consider themselves well doctors find hypertension, heart disease, diabetes, uterine cancer, and abdominal tumors. Health reports on migrant camps mention but do not emphasize either tuberculosis or venereal disease; they are not ordinarily listed as "prevalent."

One reason may be that when public-health services do reach migrant people, it is control of communicable disease, especially tuberculosis and venereal disease, that is most likely to be emphasized, and here it is that most gains have been made. It does not mean that both are not still a serious problem in the migrant group.

If crowded and unsanitary living constitutes a health menace to E.C. and his family and to the thousands of Fontanezes and Gradys across the country, there is also a characteristic inherent in migrancy itself that makes its own unique contribution to the problem of staying alive.

Mobility creates a flock of difficulties all its own.

Most United States citizens take for granted the opportunity to make use of sundry health facilities, public and private: sanitation services; dental care; medical care; hospitalization; clinics; immunizations; reporting of communicable disease; tuberculosis tests; health education and tests in schools. But migrants cannot assume that such services are available to them. The principle that what is good for the general population is good also for migrants—that migrant people should not be segregated by having special programs developed just for them—has much merit. Nevertheless, there are points at which the gap between the resident and the migrant population is so wide that something more has to be done if essential services are to reach the people who need them most.

Mobility makes a lot of difference.

About taking your young child on a journey, the American mother's mentor and friend Dr. Benjamin Spock has this to say:

If you are going to be traveling for less than 24 hours, you can prepare and refrigerate the required bottles ahead of time. Wrap the entire outer surface of the sterilizing pail and line the lid inside with about 10 layers of newspaper, tied on with string, in such a way that you can remove the top without undoing it. When it's time to go, place the bottles in the bottle rack in the pail and pack in all the ice, in chunks or cubes, that the pail will hold (chipped ice will melt too fast) . . . If you are going to be traveling several days, it's more complicated . . . talk it over with the doctor . . . Call the airline . . .

For ninety-nine one hundredths of America's young mothers Dr. Spock's advice is excellent. For Addie Grady and Dolores Fontanez it is fantastic. Doctor? Ice? Airline? They have no doctor; they have no ice; they ride in a truck; they quiet the baby with Pepsi-Cola. For them the *Popular Medical Encyclopedia,* though equally impractical, makes more sense:

Traveling with Baby: The best advice regarding travel for a small baby is—"Don't."

But Dolores and Addie have to travel with their babies in order to live, so they do.

Not only is it difficult to give your baby proper care while you are riding thirty-six hours in the back of a truck, or even in a bus, without overnight rest stops. Working in half a dozen states in the course of a season means no continuity of either health records or health services. With immunization shots there are bound to be skips and there are bound to be duplications. Some migrant children get one polio shot somewhere along the route; some get two; a few get all three. There is reason to believe that some get an interesting if ineffectual variety of shots several times over, and certainly a great many never get any at all.

Matthew Grady was a year old when the family left Georgia and went into the migrant stream. Addie and Henry Grady had no idea that anything could be done to ease the burden of his clubfoot. If a public agency had known about his deformity when he was two years old, in theory it would have been able to correct it with 24.5 consecutive weeks of treatment; when he was four, it would have taken 32.3 consecutive weeks. But no agency did find him. And, if it had, it could not have accepted the case. Why? Because the parents could not give assurance that they would have Matthew on hand for the subsequent steps of the treatment. Neither could the agency offer any guarantee or even any hope that adequate professional help would be available to carry on the treatment in the communities to which the family might go—even if the Gradys had been sure where they were going.

In addition to the practical difficulties encountered in travel, in addition to the lack of continuity of health services, mobility is responsible for another problem confronting the migrant population. They have no legal-residence status. This fact denies them the voting privilege and, more crucial to their immediate basic needs, it denies them various forms of health and welfare service. Their need qualifies them for public assistance; the laws declare them ineligible. They are residents of nowhere.

Details of residence requirements vary widely from state to state. The range is from one to five years. Hawaii and New York stand alone in making no time requirements. Since 1873 New York has provided help on basis of need without regard to residence. There have been changes in the policy for determining which unit of government pays for what kind of care and in what proportion, but the principle that need must be met has remained inviolate. At present the state, with some federal funds, pays for assistance and care of persons without one year's residence. But the issue is not dead. A bill instituting a residence requirement passed the legislature in 1960 but was vetoed by Governor Rockefeller.

The residence question, of course, affects groups other than agricultural migrants; the ratio of migrants to others varies with the conditions in a particular state. In New York migrant people who receive aid represent only a fragment of the total. Among every 60,000 persons receiving some form of public assistance in the state, just five are identified as agricultural migrant workers. Most of the aid they receive is given in some form of medical and hospital care. A smaller proportion comes under the general heading of child welfare. For a few it is listed in a special category· "Burial Only." Despite protestations of what migrants "cost," of the total number of migrants in the state, just about one in every hundred receives any kind of aid, and the public expenditure amounts to something in the neighbor-hood of $100,000. At the same time the State Department of Labor estimates migrant New York State earnings at an annual $25,000,000. Eighty-five per cent of this is spent in the com-munities in which it is earned.

In support of residence requirements, the case is made that people gravitate to a state where relief checks are forthcoming. The New York State Department of Public Welfare replies that this is not their experience. California, Florida, Michigan, Ohio, Arizona, and Maryland all have high residence require-ments, yet their net civilian in-migration far exceeds that of New York. People move to get a job, says the department, to earn more money, to be with relatives or friends, to find better schools, better places to live, a better climate; it has yet to be proved that they deliberately move in order to collect relief checks and get free medical care.

In one small state an official estimates that $100,000 of public money goes for staff time in administering the residence law, in long-distance calls and services of warnings to depart. He sug-gests that this figure may very well exceed the actual cost of the care required by the needy persons.

Private agencies resist residence requirements because when there are no public funds for emergency aid the burden falls on already overstrained private resources.

The horror of what can happen in a large-scale emergency shows up in Florida's experience in the abnormal winter of 1957–58.

Beginning on December 10, the state suffered a series of freezes, the worst since 1897. They were aggravated by torren-tial rains. Once again the hoary joke spread abroad about the man who went south for the winter and found it. The northern press reported that Florida's luxury hotels were throwing in free meals with the price of a room. In Homestead, a vegetable center southwest of Miami, soup lines two blocks long harked back to the 1930s; and twenty-five miles from the frosty glitter of Miami Beach a reporter found four small children huddled together for warmth in an eight-by-sixteen-foot frame cabin. For days they had been sharing scraps of food, but the scraps were gone. They were migrants.

Hardest hit was Immokalee, a wide place in the road in Collier County. Here the enemy was water. Farmers had replanted winter vegetables as many as four times, only to watch the water birds enjoy the lakes that should have been cornfields. Here it was that 800 migrant families—3200 persons —were subsisting in housing so makeshift that earlier in the season the employment service had refused to recruit labor for the area. The freeze and the rains destroyed the jobs, and if water was the enemy of the farmer, it was the friend of epidemic. One public-health doctor and three nurses frantically vaccinated for diphtheria.

On January 10, one month to the day after the first freeze, the President declared four Florida counties major disaster areas, meaning that they were eligible to receive surplus government foods. The wheels were slow to move. Nobody quite knew why, but the President's declaration was not reported in the press, and even concerned government agencies in Washington were weeks finding it out. On January 20 the Migrant Ministry of the National Council of Churches telegraphed the President, requesting precisely the action already taken ten days before. The New York *Times* reported the telegram as news.

The Red Cross gave some local help but was reputedly prevented from large-scale assistance by a policy of not moving in on situations of unemployment. Local communities in the stricken areas and across the state worked zealously to assemble resources, and appeals to church groups on all levels brought response. The Congregational Christian Service Committee sent in a thousand-dollar check; the Eastern Mennonite Mission Board in Pennsylvania dispatched four thousand cans of beef by truck. From women of the Presbyterian Church in the U.S. (Southern) came funds and clothing, the latter in such abundance that this particular need was actually met. Several denominations indicated that they had no machinery for handling emergency appeals.

By February 10 government surplus commodities were being distributed on a regular two-week basis to 28,000 persons in Immokalee, Belle Glade, and Pahokee and in the counties of Dade, Broward, and Palm Beach. To supplement the corn meal, flour, rice, powdered milk, and processed cheese, local migrant committees used all the funds they could get to purchase at wholesale bacon, lard, baking powder, milk for babies, and kerosene. In particularly short supply were soap and matches.

By mid-April relief came in the form of the annual spring migration up the eastern seaboard.

It is true, of course, that many state and local welfare units waive regulations in cases of dire emergency. But with the vulnerable migrant, emergency is too often chronic, and crash programs are no real solution for him, for the community, or for the state.

Nor does disaster coupled with mobility and substandard living conditions tell the whole story.

Agencies may be understaffed; they may be unaware; they may be uninterested; they may be nonexistent. Few indeed are the migrant camps that afford private clinics of the kind Dolores Fontanez found in Illinois. Migrants may never have heard of public-health services, or they may be living in a camp too isolated for them to be able to seek help. What good is a clinic if it is located in a place you can't get to or if it is open only while you are working in the fields?

Compounding these difficulties are the cultural blocks that stand in the way of organized health services. Doctors and nurses may not understand migrant behavior. A doctor gives precise directions to a Latin-American woman. She listens with attention; she smiles and answers, "*Sí, sí,*" and he takes this to mean that she will carry out his instructions to the letter. It often means that she didn't understand him at all, or it may be that it is utterly out of the question for her to take a teaspoon full of the medicine in a half glass of water every two hours while she is working a ten-hour day in tomatoes, even supposing that she ever knew what time it was; she lives not by the clock but by the sun. But in any case it is unthinkable for her to say to the doctor, "No, no"; that would be rude.

Doctors, even if accessible, are a luxury migrants have learned to do without. Neither Latin nor Negro migrants are frightened by sickness. They are used to dealing with it themselves, with home remedies; they believe their own remedies work, and sometimes they do. Negro migrants report various unfortunate experiences, real or fancied, with white doctors. The doctor has made them wait until all the white patients have been treated; he acted as if he was afraid he wouldn't get his money; he kept them coming back as long as they had any money and then he discharged them.

In spite of all these frustrations there is a positive side to the health picture. Still, the process of amelioration, the attack on root causes—these are long, tedious, discouraging, and heroic. They lack the drama of disaster.

Patient and consistent encouragement on the part of the federal Public Health Service and the Children's Bureau is bearing fruit in a number of ways.

Some states are extending immunization services to migrants. Some are naming specialists to be responsible for information and consultation on migrant health problems. In a few cases nurses are scheduling regular visits to migrant camps; sometimes staff are added at peak harvest seasons. On the eastern seaboard a seventy-two-page pamphlet listing addresses of health services in major migrant areas has become a useful tool for persons who may need to help migrant people find medical assistance:

Farm Placement personnel, social workers, schoolteachers, police, ministers. A map of the United States spotting the 943 counties having a hundred or more domestic migrants at the peak of a normal crop season enables agencies to blueprint intelligent advance planning for extension of services. A special record card has been developed and its use urged upon all health personnel working with agricultural migrants. The problem of co-ordinating services between states is being attacked by a long-term exploration and experiment with the people who migrate between Texas and Michigan.

Special migrant clinics, public and private, are by no means general, but they exist.

New Jersey has inaugurated a health clinic for migrant children in four counties during July and August. Services include polio and diphtheria shots; dental treatment; testing for tuberculosis and follow-up of positive reactors; treatment of minor colds and skin infections and referral of major conditions to appropriate treatment agencies.

For five years New York's potato-growing Steuben County has held a one-day free clinic for seasonal workers, offering chest X rays, blood testing, and immunization against polio, diphtheria, smallpox, lockjaw, whooping cough. Each year, in the course of its one-day operation, the clinic has served more than six hundred migrants. The variety of sponsoring agencies gives a clue to the degree of public and private interest and co-ordination involved in accomplishing the project: the State Department of Health; health officials of northern Steuben County; the County Public Health Association; the County Nursing Service; and the Voluntary Health Association of Steuben County.

Minnesota has begun work on tuberculosis by conducting a survey among Spanish-speaking migrants in one local setting: Hollandale, in Freeborn County in the southern part of the state. The process of even such an initial survey is not simple.

At its most effective it has to be based primarily on the use of local facilities and resources, with help from state agencies, both official and voluntary; standard procedures and record forms must be simplified; good communication with the migrant families must be arranged by securing interpreters who not only understand and speak Spanish but who can win the trust of the migrant people; thorough clearance must be obtained from local and county medical and welfare groups. There must be three stages: planning, the survey itself, and follow-up. Of these the third is at once the most important and the most difficult. The significant feature of this Hollandale survey is that it provides a model on which to begin building an effective statewide program.

A staggering aspect of migrant health services is how to get them paid for; migrant earnings obviously can cover only the most routine. Various experiments have been tried in a number of states without conspicuous success. In Wisconsin about 10 per cent of the migrant population is covered by health insurance provided by employers. The President's Committee is working with consultants from three national insurance organizations toward a pilot program for year-round family coverage for migrant people.

Gradually states are applying sanitation regulations to migrant camps. Illinois, which has twenty-one counties that employ collectively some 15,000 migrants, at long last has embarked on a two-year trial period to give growers time to improve their camps through voluntary action. Gains come about in devious ways, and it is not clear that this move of the state authorities is related to what happened to Ernesto Perez in Du Page County, but it seems likely that it is. In any event, Ernesto's story needs to be told, not only because it did result at least in immediate county action but also because it throws a spotlight on a new area of danger to migrant workers: the use of organic pesticides.

Medical authorities caution those who work with such products to avoid their cumulative effects by showering with plenty of hot water at the end of the day and washing out work clothes. One insecticide in common use and highly poisonous is parathion. Dusting a field with it, a Mexican national became ill on the job, and that night he died. In Florida twelve persons were poisoned after using sprays containing it; six of them died. Apparently neither the news of these occurrences nor the medical warnings had reached Du Page County, Illinois, whose county seat is only thirty crow-flight miles from the Chicago Loop, when one day in July a farmer had his cabbage field sprayed with parathion. The next day Ernesto Perez, son of a migrant, died from absorption of parathion through his skin. A coroner's jury met in the farmer's barn, and in the course of its deliberations it inspected the seven buildings in which thirty-seven migrants and their families were living. One was a hayloft; another—the dwelling of Bruno Perez and his family of ten—was a converted chicken shed. The accounts do not record the degree of conversion of the chicken shed or the coroner's verdict, but the event did have results in Du Page County. In August the Board of Supervisors passed an ordinance making camp operators responsible for storage and use of poisonous insecticides and setting standards for camps, including a shower head for every twenty persons. Du Page County officials believe this to be the first law of its kind in Illinois—in an oblique way a memorial to Ernesto Perez, aged two.

Related to the danger from chemicals is the whole area of farm accidents and workmen's compensation. The National Safety Council rates agriculture as the third most hazardous industry; mining and construction precede it, and transportation comes fourth. Yet only California, Hawaii, Ohio, and Puerto Rico have compulsory workmen's compensation for agricultural workers on the same basis as for other workers. Three quarters of the state workmen's compensation laws exempt agriculture from automatic coverage; in most cases voluntary coverage is possible if the employer so desires. The problem is complex, but there remains the question of whether or not farm workers should have at least the same protections as the rest of American labor.

As ambitious as any undertaking in behalf of migrant health is a Florida five-year pilot project initiated in 1956. Two years earlier the Bureau of Maternal and Child Health of the Florida State Board of Health conducted a special investigation of the health problems of migrants; out of this came the idea of a public-health team. Financed through the United States Children's Bureau, the experiment is centered in Palm Beach County. It has a double aim: to develop techniques adapted to the social and cultural patterns of the migrant people; and by using a medical social worker, a health education specialist, a nutritionist, two nurses, two practicing physicians, and a liaison worker, to demonstrate the effectiveness of the team approach. The philosophy conceives of using also the knowledge and skill of other professionals; but always the approach is to plan, not for, but with, the migrants themselves. Successful programs include family clinics, prenatal and mothers' classes, and a plan for hospital maternity care and postnatal checkup in a doctor's private office for a total cost of eighty dollars. Recognizing the crucial role of the crew leader in migrant life, the team organized a class for crew leaders; twenty came an evening a week for twelve weeks and discussed topics centering on health and chosen by themselves—with a minimum of staff guidance.

The team members believe they have demonstrated that public-health activities can be carried on successfully with the migrant group, and they declare that proverbial remarks like "You can't do anything with those people; they don't want to learn anything; they're happy the way they are" do not stand up in the face of the Florida experience.

But the proverbs go on.

Interlude:

HUMAN COMEDY

If you prick us, do we not bleed?
if you tickle us, do we not laugh?
if you poison us, do we not die?
and if you wrong us, shall we not revenge?
—*The Merchant of Venice.*

"Migrants? No, we don't have migrants here. Oh, you mean those Mexican families that come in to chop and pull bollies? They're not *migrants,* honey; they're nothing but *cotton pickers.*"

* * *

"I have no prejudice because they are migrants, nor even because they are Negroes. I simply believe that we need to take a long-range view of this problem. If we place too much emphasis on getting them into school they will grow up unwilling to do stoop labor; then where will our country be?"

* * *

"A 1938 Chevy, it was. It ran, but that was all you could say for it. I was just about to haul it to the junk yard. Yes, sir, I told him, $75.00 and she's yours. He never dickered about the price, never said does she run, just handed me the cash and off he chugged, happy as a lark. These Mexican babies sure are good for business in this town."

* * *

"They are all potentially dangerous. They don't give us any trouble here because we don't let them start anything."

* * *

"It's no use dolling up a camp for those apes. They don't appreciate it. Take Bill Baxter down the road. He piped in running water and put a sink in his cookshack, and right away first thing they pulled the pipes out of the wall and took an ax to the sink. Old Bill was so mad he called the troopers in, and they asked the crew leader how come his migrants wrecked the place. The crew leader went off and talked to his people for a long time, and then he came back and said it was this way. Seems three of the men took their wives downtown Saturday night and all six of them went right into the Washington Hotel and tried to go on into the dining room. For dinner! They got turned away, of course. So they went straight back to camp and busted up the new sink. What's the sense to that?"

* * *

"Out of our own pockets we fixed up a dance hall for them so they'd have a place of their own. And we see to it that no white people go there. We really like the Mexicans here; some of them are nice boys."

* * *

"It's because our jail isn't big enough to handle them. Oh my, yes, didn't you know? The number-one migrant problem is drinking. So our little community has taken over this old freight house and put in cots and toilets. No, they don't live there; it's to take care of the ones who get really unfit to be on the street. You see there are hundreds of them all through the county. It works like this. The sugar company contracts with the farmers to buy their sugar beets, and it's really the company that brings the migrants in as part of the deal. They turn up when the beet season opens, and mostly they live around on the farms. The farmer finds some little old building for them; beet huts, we call them. I don't suppose they're very good. Our mayor tells me the sugar company and the government people are trying to persuade the farmers to fix up their beet huts, but the mayor says what really has worked is a couple of cases where the migrants themselves told the farmer they wouldn't come back to work another year unless they got a better place to live. Isn't that kind of cute? It just goes to show they're human."

* * *

"We raised our share the easiest way. All we did was collect old clothes and take them out to that migrant camp at Queens Crossing. You should see what those people will pay seventy-five cents for. More fun! We made $45.00 in forty-five minutes, and it wasn't a good time to go, either, because the people hadn't been working for three days and they didn't have too much cash. We gave the crew leader five dollars for their welfare fund."

* * *

"I often wonder what they do on Sundays, why we see so few of them in church."

14. SCHOOL FOR A BEAN PICKER

> When the classroom door opens to admit a new child in the middle of the school year and in the middle of the lesson, this is what the teacher must understand: "Unless this child finds opportunity here, he will find it nowhere. His education is the sum total of temporary school stops in classrooms like this, always at the busy time of the year. It can be no better than what I offer him now, for whatever time he is here."
> —*Teaching Children Who Move with the Crops;* *Fresno County Schools, California.*

The teachers agreed that the six-week summer session had been a satisfying experience.

"Why?" asked the principal.

There were several replies.

"The children were really glad to come."

"You could watch their fears disappear as they began to understand that they belonged here, that this school was theirs."

"The classes were small enough so we could work with each child at his own level."

"Their experience is so limited that every little thing we did with them became a means of learning something."

"We could emphasize living together and feel fairly sure there would be a carry-over to the family situation."

"We could deliberately plan to build attitudes—and sometimes see it work."

They would like to do it again, the teachers decided, if for no other reason than the chance to have another child like Howard.

Thin and undersized for his thirteen years, Howard turned up at school one noon and asked if he might stay. He couldn't ever get there before twelve, he explained haltingly. He had to work from six o'clock till eleven in potatoes. The age range of the school was supposed to be five to twelve, but the staff decided to make an exception of Howard. From that day until the end of the session, after his five hours in the potato fields, Howard walked the four and a half miles to school. He was vague about where and when he had been to school before, and it soon became clear that he could not read. By the end of the summer he had learned to read; he had gained five pounds; and eight times out of ten he could send the ball into the basket.

This was back in 1948, at Freehold, New Jersey. Fifty miles from Times Square, and the center of New Jersey's ten-million-dollar tri-county potato region—Monmouth, Middlesex, and Mercer counties—Freehold had then just 7500 people but a surprising diversity of interests: it manufactured carpets, coats, dresses, pickles, instant coffee, and whisky; it was the site of the county courthouse, a race track, and the spring where Molly Pitcher drew water for the American soldiers at the Battle of Monmouth. In 1947 Freehold acquired another attraction: an experimental summer school for migrant children.

The idea of such a school moved toward reality when the New Jersey Migrant Labor Board and the State Department of Education together drafted an amendment to the state school law, extending the privilege of public education to the children of migrant workers. The legislature passed the amendment; the governor signed it, and the Migrant Labor Division of the Department of Labor and Industry inaugurated the Freehold experiment.

All this did not mean that the community had no share in the school. The Board of Education made a building available. The Red Cross provided daily transportation for the cateress who prepared the hot lunch for the children. The county library sent in reading books for the children to borrow and take home. The county social-service organization gave counsel and aid in special cases. And with the daily milk order the local dairy sent free ice.

The following winter, casting around for a suitable location for a second school, the Migrant Labor Board found two communities where the way seemed to be clear. Then opposition arose from the local Parent Teachers' Associations. So in 1948 New Jersey's one migrant school again opened in Freehold. This was the year that Howard appeared.

By 1959 there were three migrant summer schools in New Jersey, serving 158 children: 63 at Cranbury, 54 at Fairton, and 41 at Freehold. The cost to the state for the three schools—salaries, rent, transportation, food, supplies—was $12,400; from the national school lunch program and the special school milk program the state received reimbursement of $300.

State inspectors report some 1600 migrant children in the state each summer; the schools reach one in ten. Nevertheless, they do demonstrate what can be done.

Other states have experimented with the special migrant-school idea: Colorado, Pennsylvania, Michigan, New York, Oregon, Ohio, California. Voluntary organizations, notably the National Child Labor Committee and the Consumers League, have contributed counsel and financial help. Some private agencies have sponsored schools of their own, such as the American Association of University Women in Des Plaines, Illinois, and the Roman Catholic Diocese of Crookston, Minnesota, where Texas Latin families come to the Red River Valley to work in sugar beets. The Migrant Ministry of the National Council of Churches has been a pioneer in a dozen states. For one example, its pilot schools at Hamilton, in 1951 and King Ferry in 1952, both in New York, stimulated the state to embark on a similar program. Today New York has four migrant summer schools.

But always there are too few special schools to make a dent in the total need. Though immeasurably valuable for the children whom they do reach, the special schools are at best expensive and fragmentary supplements to a broader concept: the policy of opening doors of public schools to migrant children wherever they happen to go. More doors are open and they are open wider than they used to be, but the layman should not be misled into believing this to be a simple solution to educating migrant children. The difficulties are legion.

A mid-term influx of children finds classrooms already bursting at the seams. There is a shortage of books and supplies and no money in the school budget to buy more. The newcomers appear in the middle of a study unit for which they have no preparation. Few of them bring school records, and when they do the record often either reveals little or serves as a prejudicial handicap. Practically all the children are retarded anywhere from one to five years. Standard tests are difficult to use in grading them because their vocabularies are so limited. One class did poorly in an intelligence test with the word "chimney" in it; as it developed, they knew very well what a chimney was only they called it a smoke pipe. The Latin children speak little English, and the southern Negroes have a soft drawl that northern teachers have to learn to understand. One teacher tells of the trouble she had getting the class to master addition. They were all quick at arithmetic because they were used to figuring piecework earnings, but they could not learn to "carry one."

Finally a small voice suggested, "Teacher, do you mean we *tote* one?"

The length of their stay is problematical, their attendance spotty. The parents feel that the children must work in the fields to augment the family income; or they must stay home in camp to baby-sit; or they don't have school clothes, or they haven't any shoes; or the parents don't see that going to school has helped the older children to earn any more money than they did before they went to school, so why send the younger ones?

The local superintendent fears criticism from the community if he admits migrant children. The National Farm Bureau recommends to its state units that local school facilities be made available to children of migratory farm workers, but this is not yet the uniform position of local farm groups or of all individual growers.

"Our farm members don't think there is any problem in this county about education of migrant children," explained one official. And in Berrien County, Michigan, when a group of national agencies wanted to collect data on migrant education, a farm group blocked the project on the ground that "studies pertaining to migrant labor always result in unfavorable publicity for growers."

Are migrant children educable? The answer is yes, and it is readily substantiated by reports from the summer schools. In Wiggins, Colorado, in the summer of 1956, in a seven-week session, Stanford Achievement Tests showed an average gain of five and a half months—although the teachers were inclined to find it just as significant that during the same period Miguel Elizondo gained five pounds.

"The cause of retardation—sixty-seven per cent in our Colorado migrants—is centered in lack of school attendance," states Alfred M. Potts of the Colorado State Department of Education. "It definitely is not due to lack of scholastic ability. Studies show these children to have about the same ratio of slow learners, average-intelligence groups, and potentially superior children as other population groups."

Dr. Frank Mann of the State Teachers College in Towson, Maryland, retained by the Pennsylvania State University to direct its model migrant summer school in Potter County, bears this out:

"During four summers we have discovered the same range of abilities among these children—they suffer from two to five years retardation—as one might expect to find among any other group of similar size, with the level of achievement closely correlated with school attendance." Retardation increases in direct proportion to the number of years in migrancy and the number of moves made each year.

Here and there the old pattern of crop vacations persists. When the strawberries are ready for picking, schools close, and the time is made up later in the summer. But by that time the migrant children have moved on.

Is education of migrant children a local responsibility?

A desperate school superintendent in Texas poured out his problem in a letter to his United States senator; for good measure he sent the same letter to his congressman, to the President's Committee on Migratory Labor, and to the United States Office of Education. Bureaucracy was working, and the first three letters were promptly forwarded to Education.

His school had a registration of 2700 children, he explained; of these 1300 were migrants, who came in after school had been going for some seven weeks. None stayed to finish the year.

"Most of them call this city home," he continued. "We feel we should be entitled to some aid, the same as army posts. It appears that we are educating children for other states at our expense."

At least eight states now allot additional funds to local school districts admitting migrant children into their schools. The state of Pennsylvania gives one dollar a day to local school districts for each migrant child who attends, but superintendents of affected schools say this is not enough. A precedent for federal aid exists in Public Law 874, which authorizes financial assistance to local educational agencies "where the United States Government has placed financial burdens." How extensive such aid would be if the principle were applied to migrant areas is a guess; the United States Office of Education estimates that some 600,000 children are affected by family migrancy in agriculture.

Intelligent consideration of the problem of educating migrant children cannot fail to take into account the fabric of migrant life. Child labor is wrapped tightly around educational opportunity, and so are substandard earnings. So is the problem of day care for young children. So is deficient nutrition, which limits attention span and comprehension. So are community attitudes.

The answers are obvious but not easy. The public school must assume responsibility for the education of every child within its jurisdiction. This principle must hold true no matter how short the child's stay, how difficult his language problem, how different his cultural background, how great the retardation his parents' migrancy has caused. Teachers must look at migrant children not with surprise but with welcome, accepting their presence in the schoolroom as a normal event. Curricula must be child-centered and flexible, so that even a migrant may find his way in them. Testing must be conducted within the framework of the migrant child's experience. Some procedure must be worked out for transmittal of school records; and the records must be of such an interpretive nature as not to militate against the child in the new situation. There must be a school lunch program, and there must be health services. The school must work with growers and recruiting agencies to get from crew leaders, labor contractors, and families advance information on numbers of children expected to arrive and the probable duration of their stay. The local school district must have state and federal assistance. Child labor in agriculture must be regulated.

Special schools have a supplementary role. They are justified in so far as they overcome retardation; meet problems of language and cultural difference; demonstrate the educability of migrant children; experiment with techniques and curricula to meet the felt needs of the migrant children; provide a constructive alternative to unsupervised idleness; fill gaps in the school calendar created by mobility and crop vacations.

All this is much more readily said than accomplished, and even if all of it were done everywhere, it is too true that, so long as the child migrates, his chance for a sound education is not good.

Nevertheless, the climate is better than it was a decade ago. Encouraging news comes from scattered locations, and it takes various forms.

Colleges and universities are offering workshops for teachers who have migrant children in their classes; for example, Florida State College in Tallahassee, Arizona State College in Tempe, and Adams State College in Alamosa, Colorado. From the last has come *Learning on the Move*, a teacher handbook.

The Texas legislature has authorized a special pre-school program for non-English-speaking children.

The University of Wisconsin and the U. S. Office of Education have conducted a study from which they are developing guidelines for any state wanting to educate its migrant children —how to locate the children, how to create curricula to meet their needs, how to finance their education.

Each spring and fall in New Jersey close to five hundred migrant children—nearly a third of those in the state—enroll in some seventy public schools and attend for a few weeks.

California, Arizona, and Florida have some excellent schools populated entirely with migrant children. In California a predominantly migrant school discourages dropouts by enlisting teachers, nurses, cafeteria workers, and people from the community to discuss with seventh graders job opportunities and the importance of educational preparation.

Vermont has only a few hundred apple pickers, but their presence from mid-September well into the third week of October cuts into the school year. One school board secured a legal opinion that migrant children could be declared non-resident; State Education Commissioner A. John Holden, Jr., scotched this with an unequivocal statement:

In a case where a family is in town, even temporarily, for the purpose of earning a living such as working in a harvest, that town is properly the family's residence for school purposes during the time, and the children are entitled to go to school there on the same basis as children who live there the year round.

Five school districts later reported having migrant pupils enrolled on the same basis as other children.

Asked how the southern Negro migrant children were fitting into his consolidated school, a principal in western New York said:

"They don't make us any more problems than any other children. Unless you call it special that one mother from town told me her little girl came home in tears because she didn't have any migrants in her class. And we've got one boy in high school. I told his crew leader he'd have to find work here for that family anyway through the second Saturday in November; we'll have a riot on our hands for sure if he takes Calvin back down south before we play Ulysses Central. That boy just carries our football team on his back."

Postlude:

THE GRADY FAMILY

And God smiled again,
And the rainbow appeared,
And curled itself around His shoulder.
—*James Weldon Johnson,* The Creation *from*
God's Trombones, *Viking Press.*

The afternoon she and Henry each brought home a family
present became the first time Addie felt certain it wasn't a
dream.

They had done it; they were settled down. Maybe you
couldn't say it was a house, but it had three rooms and it was
sure enough home.

What it was, it was a bus with the insides pulled out and the
wheels gone, and it sat right there on the ground in a pear
orchard, just as firm as though it grew straight up from roots.
It was painted gray with a neat red trim, and it had electric
lights and good cold water piped inside. All told, there were
sixteen buses in that camp, eight in a lengthwise line running
back from the road alongside the pear orchard, and then you
turned a corner and eight more buses ran behind the orchard

parallel to the road. Coming in from the highway, you stopped at the fourth bus down and that was the Gradys'.

They came there from Willow Brook in August. They worked in peaches awhile, and then apples began to come along. They had to pay rent, $3.50 a week. It seemed a lot when you thought about how there wasn't any rent at all at Willow Brook, nothing at all to pay there; but Willow Brook was a dump. For advantages you should expect to pay.

"We're lucky, that's what," the woman in the next bus but one told Addie.

Her name was Mrs. Sinclair and she was fat and comfortable. She wore a little round white hat with red letters on it that said *Life Is Just a Bowl of* and then painted right on the hat was a bunch of red cherries. Matthew did love that hat, and Mrs. Sinclair told him when she died he could have it. So Matthew took to saying every time he saw her, "How do you feel today, Mrs. Sinclair?" And she would say, "Right good, Mr. Matthew. You got a long time to wait."

Here's what Mrs. Sinclair said:

"We just came up from Suffolk County, and you know what down there? We had to pay $3.00 a week per person—not per family, per *person*—for nothing you could call facilities, a place not half this good, not by half. We're lucky."

When September came Mr. Elliott (he was the nearest like Mr. Wilson of anybody they'd met since Georgia), he came around on Labor Day and said to have the children ready on Wednesday, ten minutes of eight for sure, the school bus would be along. So Roosevelt and Sister and Matthew (Matthew turned six in August), off they went to school in the bus right along with the children that belonged.

It all came about so natural.

One day Lottie never said a word, just took herself off from apples and went into town and got fixed up to study to be a nurse in the hospital, sleep and eat there and everything.

Next thing Lottie came out one night to visit and said there's a job down there at that hospital, Addie, why don't you try for it? Cleaning, eight hours, six days, steady; the bus to town stops right up here on the highway. Addie thought right away of Princess Anne and said no, she couldn't, but Lottie said I already told them about Princess Anne and they said bring her along, if she's good we don't care, we'll try it anyway. So Addie went, and she got the job.

When the apples finished, if Henry didn't get himself work in the fertilizer plant; they didn't say it would be steady, more like a spell now and then, but while it lasted it was work.

And Mr. Elliott said, you folks aim to stay here through the winter? Nobody has yet; we get snowbanks; you'll need a shovel to get you out to the highway, but I don't know why you shouldn't try it if you want to. And he brought them in the cutest little potbellied wood-burning stove to keep warm by, and he pushed up a couple of old pear trees and said you're doing me a favor to chop up this wood and burn it. Then he said, I don't like snow much myself, not any more. I'm getting too old. The wife and I'll be going off to Florida pretty soon, so don't be surprised if I don't come around to collect rent again much before spring. Just make yourselves easy and don't freeze up.

It was coming by the newspaper office that she saw it in the window, a black tin frame with white letters that you could slide in to spell a name or anything you wanted. The newspaperman helped her fix it up. It took two frames to say it, and this is how it looked:

GRADY RESI
DENCE

They could put it right on the bus door.

She had just finished tacking it up when Henry came along, lugging his bundle. He laughed when he saw the sign, and then he handed her his package. It was bulky. Addie ripped off the paper.

It was a silver-colored rural-delivery mailbox, with letters black and plain:

GRADY

Friends of

the Harvesters

15. THE MIGRANT MINISTRY

The Migrant Ministry is transitory. It erects no permanent buildings, creates no permanent organizations. Its state is always precarious. It touches a life that is here today and gone tomorrow. It sows, but it never knows where the harvest will be gathered nor what the fruit will be. It knows only that there is human need that cries out for healing.

—*Hermann N. Morse, Board of National Missions, United Presbyterian Church, U.S.A.*

The decade of the thirties blew a bitter wind. It churned into a dust bowl the farming counties of Oklahoma and Arkansas, of Missouri and Kansas and Texas. The gaunt harvest of those hungry years tractored out the marginal farmer, the tenant, the southern sharecropper. Into the millions the migrant population swelled. Community resentment flared.

The nation reaped the whirlwind. At state borders bum blockades appeared, manned in California by the Los Angeles police; in Colorado by the militia; by state authorities in Florida and in New Jersey, where Negro migrants coming in for potato harvest were turned back at the Delaware River. Counties took measures to prevent migrant labor from lingering long enough to qualify for relief. At the close of the 1934 pea harvest California's San Luis Obispo County voted $2500 to furnish pea pickers with enough gasoline and food to get them into the next county. The authorities there sent back word that if the performance were repeated, the migrants would be met at the county line with guns.

Yet in the San Joaquin Valley in 1936 a county doctor was able to say, "We used to discover conditions in migrant camps after they became tragedy; today, together, we are preventing tragedy."

By "together" he meant his own county health department and a missionary nurse employed to serve in migrant camps. Her sponsor was an interdenominational agency then known as the Council of Women for Home Missions.

In time the women's council surrendered its identity in a series of agency mergers; today the work of Protestant groups in migrant camps is known as the Migrant Ministry. Nationally it is administered from the Division of Home Missions of the National Council of Churches. It receives support from some twenty denominations; in thirty-four states councils of churches, councils of church women, and a network of committees sponsor social and religious programs in migrant camps, all as part of the Migrant Ministry.

It began soon after World War I, when the Interchurch World Movement of North America conducted a survey of migrant farm labor on the east coast. Added to the hardship of irregular work and low pay, the survey found "the very acute problem of housing, sanitation, and morals"; it recommended "trained workers directed by some joint agency of the churches" and "itinerant missionaries who would follow the migratory movement itself as counsellors and companions of the transient workers."

The summer of 1920 saw four centers set up to give daytime care to children whose parents were cutting asparagus and picking tomatoes and peppers in the fields of the eastern seaboard. At Riverton, New Jersey, and Houston, Delaware, the pickers were Italian; at Bel Air and Preston, Maryland, they were Polish. All of them were migrants, living for the duration of the picking season in cannery camps or in shacks on vegetable farms.

The young director of the centers had been educated at Ward Belmont in Nashville and the University of Oregon, both of them a far cry from migrant labor on the eastern shore of the Chesapeake. But Lila Bell Acheson had energy, enthusiasm, and imagination. In later years these qualities assisted her to become, with her husband, founder, editor, and owner of the *Reader's Digest*; in 1920 they enlisted for her the co-operation of growers and canners and community leaders in behalf of migrant children. At Riverton the community secured the use of a school building, raised a hundred dollars for incidentals, collected baby clothes and crib blankets and dishes, and drove from shack to shack in the early-morning hours collecting the children and delivering them to the center. At Bel Air cannery owner W. E. Robinson spent $500 putting a building in condition and piping in running water. At Newark, Delaware, the president of the United Canneries Corporation said, "We've got to have a center here; last year we paid a man thirty dollars a week just to keep the children off the railroad tracks."

The third summer, for eleven weeks, twenty workers fed and cared for 199 children; the time seemed longer than the days the calendar recorded, because each of the six centers opened at dawn and closed long after dark.

By 1924 the word had spread to Oregon, and the result was a series of day camps for children of hoppickers at Salem, apple pickers in the Hood River Valley, and berrypickers at Gresham.

In California, with its twelve-month growing season and its permanently migrating labor force of uncounted thousands, the dearth of health services loomed as the acute need. There were no nurses in migrant camps. In co-operation with the state departments of health and education the women hammered out details of a program; they secured grower co-operation, and in January 1926 the first nurse went in to the Imperial Valley to work with Mexican cotton pickers.

Two years later a nurse named Eva Barnes joined the staff and went first to work among Japanese asparagus cutters in the Sacramento Delta. As she moved on into the San Joaquin Valley, she found twenty-eight nationalities, not counting gypsies.

During her nurse's training Eva had set her sights on the foreign mission field, but the Presbyterian Board of Foreign Missions turned her down because she had a heart murmur. The Presbyterians need not have been put off by this detail.

In her battered *Chevrolita*, Eva Barnes regularly visited twenty-three camps. Seven o'clock each morning found her packing up her medicine kit, clothing, magazines, toys, and her lunch (a sandwich, milk, an apple). A monthly report itemizes 259 camp visits, 1850 family calls, contacts with 5795 individual migrants, and treatment of 34 scabies, 314 infections, 119 colds, 117 pregnant mothers, and 19 cases of venereal disease. Camp visits were interspersed with clinics, mothers' clubs, first-aid classes, children's story hours.

Her daily routine became a series of crises.

A child died of croup. Eva Barnes notified the coroner, comforted the family, made arrangements for the funeral.

At the next camp a mother rushed out to meet her car.

"We had a fight. Juan is hurt and Pete has gone to jail. Come quick."

At the third stop a crowd of mothers were waiting for her.

"My Lupe is pink all over and she swallows up."

"My husband is all over sores. You come."

She went and found two well-developed cases of smallpox. Not being very uncomfortable, the older patient had just been around visiting all the other campers. The circumstances called for general quarantine, isolation of the patient, segregation of the family in new living quarters. These accomplished, Eva Barnes walked toward her car, only to be waylaid by a dozen children: "Miss Barnes, tell us a story."

She worked closely with public agencies, and like Lila Bell Acheson, Eva Barnes had a gift for enlisting active aid from the community. She cites examples: three canneries, three general practitioners, a Korean dentist, a Japanese nurse, the Red Cross, the Boy Scouts, the P.T.A., any number of teachers, and the Women's Missionary Federation of Sacramento.

By the close of the 1930s the Migrant Ministry was working in fifteen states: Maryland, Delaware, New Jersey, Connecticut, Pennsylvania, New York; Ohio and Michigan; Florida, Louisiana, and Arkansas; and Colorado, Arizona, California, and Oregon. By no means was it relieving all the ills of migrancy for all the migrants, but it was demonstrating that something could be done. Its catalytic role began to come clear.

Through the Emergency Relief Administration the state departments of education in New York and New Jersey assigned unemployed teachers to work under the direction of the Migrant Ministry.

Authorities of the Farm Security Administration, responsible for developing a series of federal farm-labor camps, saw the Migrant Ministry child-care center at Belle Glade, Florida. They said, "This is good; this we must do," and forthwith they incorporated such centers into their program.

The California Board of Health placed a physician and two nurses at the disposal of the women's council to set up clinics in migrant camps.

Federal funds were made available to the Migrant Ministry to expand migrant child care in New York State. When in 1946 a change in legislation discontinued the funds, the state took over the program, and it continues it today, though even now the state has centers for only a fraction of its migrant children.

The demonstration role has not outlived itself. Arizona is only one of several states where there are scores of migrant settlements —often aggregates of tar paper and billboard hovels located outside the bounds of any incorporated community—with no public services of any kind. Harold Lundgren, Arizona Migrant Ministry director, is not one to pull his punches. Far and wide he reported in accurate and colorful detail some of the health needs he had seen. Word reached the Phoenix Kiwanis Club, and the Kiwanians gave him a check for $1500. He bought a second-hand trailer and converted in into a mobile clinic. One who came within earshot of the story was a retired doctor; he had migrated from practice in a cold north country to relax through his declining years in Arizona sunshine. Lundgren successfully killed whatever attraction the doctor's new-found leisure held for him. Like an old fire horse the doctor took the bit between his teeth. He dusted off his stethoscope, passed the state medical board examinations, secured his Arizona license, and became the full-time volunteer head of the mobile clinic. His staff consists of a nurse, also a volunteer, and assorted housewives who give what time they can. Latin mothers and their babies are the clinic's steadiest patrons, and the sight of them waiting in a cluster outside the trailer has stirred up a lot of public curiosity that quickly becomes interest and a desire to help. Doctors have taken to donating sample medicines in enormous quantities (a mixed blessing, since the remedies do not always fit the prevailing ailments). Experience has shown the service to be most effective when the unit stays three or four weeks in the same location. Results to date: a host of people are aware of the problem, and one community has organized a clinic of its own.

Allied to the demonstration role is the function of referral. Migrant Ministry staff become versed in health and welfare resources, public and private; they know where to get emergency help, and they get it.

Because it is the only national organization that has worked consistently through the years directly with migrant people themselves in the camps where they live, the staff has become an informational resource for public agencies and a liaison between health and welfare personnel and the migrant people. They explain to the migrants what it means to be tested for tuberculosis and why it is important; they interpret social security; they encourage school boards to open schools to migrants and they persuade parents to send their children to school. They mobilize community resources, and they attack the prickly problem of converting community attitudes from indifference and hostility to acceptance and welcome.

In the thirty-four states where the Migrant Ministry now serves, the permanent staff of forty is augmented by 500 seasonal workers—doctors, nurses, teachers, students—and by 8000 community volunteers. In one way or another it aids an estimated 150,000 migrant persons.

The work takes many forms: child-care centers, mothers' clubs, all kinds of recreation, English and literacy classes, religious services, experiments with vocational training, migrant hospitality rooms in downtown store fronts.

In the course of its history the Migrant Ministry has passed two major landmarks, a twenty-fifth anniversary in 1945 and a fortieth in 1960.

The first of these it observed by launching a drive for funds to provide a fleet of mobile units. Today there are some forty of these; in a year's time they travel a hundred thousand miles and take quite a beating. Called "Harvesters," these units are simply station wagons equipped with public-address system, record player, screen and film projector, child-sized housekeeping outfits, sewing machine, balls and bats and horseshoes and checkers, first-aid kit, portable organ and chaplain's folding altar. As the fleet has grown, it has become apparent that the Harvester's practical value is matched by its symbolic significance. Not only does it identify the Migrant Ministry to the people it is intended to serve; it also dramatizes the program and the problem to the communities through which it migrates.

When the fortieth anniversary came along, the Ministry decided to mark the occasion with a self-examination in the light of changing conditions. The evaluation became a year-long process, culminating in a national conference in Washington, where 250 delegates included 150 committee members from 32 states and 50 consultants from public and private agencies.

An objective review of the self-study findings reveals an organism with enormous vitality; with a broad base of interest; with a sound working philosophy of local, state, and national participation; with an impressive body of experience in working directly with migrant people.

A persuasive indication of strength lies in the degree to which state and local committees accept high standards of performance as a working principle. There is healthy and candid admission that performance does not match proclamation, and there is realistic scrutiny of existing goals. The committees ask themselves questions like these:

Schools and child-care centers should meet state certification standards; yet if these are impossible within budgetary limitations, which is better: for us to do something that falls short or to do nothing?

Techniques must be found for enlisting migrant people themselves in the process of planning and developing programs. But is this possible in the migrant situation? Does the fact that it is so difficult suggest that we should shift the locale of the service from migrant camp to home base? If so, what happens to the people with no home base? Should the focus be limited to helping the people help themselves out of the trap of migrancy?

The preaching and teaching of religion should be geared to migrant experience and understanding. What are some reasonable criteria for measuring relevant preaching? How can we be sure that we are touching the deep spiritual needs of our people?

Volunteers should be oriented to a sympathetic understanding of cultural difference. Why are we more successful at enlisting volunteers than we are at training them? Should we do more rigid screening? What would it take to improve our training of volunteers?

On the subject of social action, considerable tension emerged. Everybody was against sin: housing and sanitation, transportation, and the activities of crew leaders should be regulated; health and welfare services and educational opportunity should be available to all migrants; some kind of minimum wage for agriculture would be desirable; imported labor should not be allowed to depress domestic wages. But there was not universal agreement that all residence laws should be abolished, nor was there consensus about which legislation should be state and which should be federal.

How aggressively and loudly should the Migrant Ministry work for legislative reform? There has been more than one instance when a committee has taken a public stand on a housing and sanitation law, or minimum wage, or enforcement of a child-labor regulation, only to find itself forbidden by a grower to work in a particular camp. Comments from state chairmen reveal a sensitivity derived from experience:

Some of our committee members are living on farms. Their opinions are based on actual experience with farm labor. Most are against legislation by state or federal government.

Farmers welcome the Migrant Ministry only when they are sure the purpose is not to get information and use it to influence legislation that would result in increased cost of farm production.

Tobacco company very sensitive to all forms of public relations. Resist any efforts to effect change. Farmers disturbed over attempts to regulate their activities in respect to agricultural labor.

One camp with an armed guard at the entrance now insists that the Migrant Ministry chaplain report to the guard his reasons for entering the camp at each visit.

Much church leadership is afraid to approach topics they feel their people might have controversy about.

National church policy stands firm on the controversial issues. They are spelled out in a statement adopted by the National Council of Churches in 1951 and calling for inclusion of agriculture under labor legislation and minimum wage; for a federal housing code for migrant camps; for extension of health and welfare services to migrants regardless of their lack of residence; for discouragement of foreign labor importation. In February 1960 the National Council took a more specific stand on Public Law 78, calling for its extension only in amended form, with provision for annual reduction in numbers and a specified date for final termination.

It is in state and local migrant committees that the repercussions hit hardest. Here it is that the choice often seems to lie between direct service to people and outspoken support for legislative reform. National Migrant Ministry policy holds that both should be done; that the cases where the program has been stopped are shocking but not prevalent; that in such cases it becomes possible in succeeding seasons for services to be reinstated.

The slowly broadening base of grass-roots participation and support does not imply a minimal role for national leadership. Edith Lowry joined the staff in 1926 and has directed the migrant work of the churches since 1928; behind her gentle blue eyes lie imagination, courage, compassion, a keen intelligence, tenacity, and extraordinary skill at resolving diverse viewpoints. More than any other one person, it is she who has fostered the concept of mobilizing all resources to focus on the problem, an approach that prompted a Colorado educator to say: "The

Migrant Ministry has created for itself the enviable position of powerful community-stimulating leadership that can make people everywhere conscious of society's responsibilities to the minority group."

For the gains that have come about through the years Edith Lowry is quick to pay primary tribute to community leadership and to public and private agencies:

"I never cease to marvel at the dedication of the people we work with. They want no credit for their agencies or for themselves; all they want to do is to contribute to the need, and they go the second and third mile to do it."

Future of the Harvesters

16. THE MAN AND
THE MACHINE

. . . we regard migrancy as one of the more
painful symptoms of present disorder in the farm
labor market, and we view its eventual extirpa-
tion as one of the more desirable consequences
which will flow from the organization of farm
labor.

                    —*AFL-CIO Agricultural Workers*
                        Organizing Committee, 1959.

In a field outside Walnut Grove, California, a group of
Sacramento Valley farmers, canners, agricultural scientists, and
newspapermen stood in the sun and watched a steel giant thirty
feet long inch its way through the dirt. It straddled a row of
tomato plants; at its front a blade cut off the plants at root
level. Spikes seized the vines; a conveyor raised them up to meet
a series of shimmying claws that grabbed the stems and shook
off the tomatoes. The stripped vines fell to the ground. The
tomatoes were caught in a troth and rolled forward to crossbelts.
which carried them laterally to crews of human sorters riding on
either side of the machine. As hands pulled out and cast away
the culls, conveyors dumped the survivors into thousand-pound
bins moving by tractor alongside the harvesting machine.

The demonstration on the Heringer ranch that September

day in 1960 was an experiment with a machine built by the
Blackwelder Manufacturing Company of Rio Vista, according to
a design developed by faculty members of the University of
California on its Davis campus; the project was subsidized by
a grant-in-aid from the California Tomato Growers Association.
Thirteen men rode the machine; watchers estimated that it
would take sixty hand pickers to perform the same work in the
same length of time. Once in quantity production, the tomato
harvester should retail at somewhere around $12,000.

Presently the machine has its disadvantages. It is practical
only for pear-shaped tomatoes, which make up just a tenth of
the California tomato crop. The University of California has for
years been working at breeding a new strain of round tomato
firm enough to withstand machine treatment, to date without
success. The mechanical harvesting process leaves a fifth of the
crop on the ground; but tomato growers figure that if minimum-
wage scales should be applied to stoop labor, the machine ought
to be a bargain even if it could salvage only 70 per cent of the
crop.

All this is important to the economy of California. Of her
wide variety of fruits, nuts, and vegetables, tomatoes represent
her largest canning crop; 60 per cent of the tomatoes grown in
the whole of the United States are raised in California.

To domestic migrants and to Mexican nationals the implica-
tion of a mechanized tomato harvest is more than important; it
is crucial. It threatens their jobs. In behalf of domestic workers,
organized labor has been vocal in its opposition to Public Law 78
on the ground that the importation program relieves the grower
of the necessity of offering decent living and working conditions
to domestic labor. The AFL-CIO Agricultural Workers Organizing Committee, which set up headquarters in Stockton in the
Sacramento Valley in 1959, not unreasonably regards this 1960
demonstration of the harvester as the tomato industry's retort to
union activities;—as if the tomato growers were saying:

"So you're pushing to get our braceros taken away from us? So you're agitating to make us offer higher piece rates to good-for-nothing domestic labor? All right, we'll mechanize. The bracero can go back to Mexico and stay there. Nobody will be paying tomato piece rates to anybody, and your domestic labor will be right where it is now—on relief."

As tomatoes are to California, so, on a smaller scale, are beans to the eastern seaboard. In New York eighty thousand tons of snap beans grown on 46,000 acres bring in some eight and a quarter million dollars. String beans we used to call them, but agricultural geneticists long ago eliminated the string. To develop a new species takes from ten to fifteen years; looking toward mechanization, plant breeders have been working for some time to get a snap-bean plant whose bearing habits would produce beans that would ripen all at once. In due time the scientists achieved one whose beans matured simultaneously in one beautiful cluster, only to find that agricultural engineers had come up with a machine whose teeth bypassed the cluster and nipped hungrily down the plant, looking for beans at appropriate intervals. The patient plant breeders went back to work.

Meantime one mechanical bean picker is slowly moving out of the experimental stage. Designed by John Ward, a grower and custom canner of Vernon, New York, and manufactured by the Chisholm-Ryder Company of Niagara Falls, it retails for under $12,000. It has not yet taken over the crop; but the push given to mechanization in California by the threat of union activity has its counterpart in the East with every step up in state housing inspection and tightened regulations. Some 150 mechanical bean pickers now harvest roughly half of the beans in New York State.

The bean harvester, too, is not without its shortcomings. For machine harvesting the rows must be planted thirty-six inches apart as against a thirty-inch space for hand picking, and when the machine has been once over the field, there is no chance for second or third pickings to catch the later-ripening pods. These two facts mean a lower yield. Machine-picked beans are bruised by the revolving teeth that begin at the top of the plant and bite their way downward; the fresh market is not receptive to beans machine-picked and bulk-handled, and hand-picked beans command a premium market price. When they reach their peak, beans need to be picked within twenty-four hours; in wet soil the mechanical picker bogs down and stubbornly refuses to function, while the grower sends out frantic calls for hand labor and the beans quietly rot. One grower tried a machine on fifty of his seven hundred acres and figured that, taking all the factors into account, the cash returns from the two methods were about even; but he still has his investment in migrant family housing, and he likes to keep labor on hand to use when the ground is wet and to do one early picking ahead of the machine. Growers who raise diversified crops demanding stoop labor will let their bean harvesters lie idle and put their migrants to work on beans in order to hold the people over for whatever crop ripens next.

Mechanization moves faster in some parts of the country than it does in others; interesting regional variations show up in cotton. When labor shortage was acute during World War II, mechanical cotton harvesters began to come into use, but they were slow to catch on. By 1950 just 4 per cent of the national cotton crop was being picked by machine; five years later, when the national figure had climbed to 23 per cent, the regional picture looked like this:

Cotton Harvested Mechanically
in 1955

California	66%
Arizona	47%
Delta States	25% to 40%
Southeast	2% to 3%

Today about one third of the national cotton crop is machine harvested.

Numerous factors contribute both to the slow rate at which cotton mechanization is taking hold and to the regional differences. In the Mississippi Delta wet weather, high humidity, rank growth of the cotton plant, and weeds impede the operation of the machine; often the cotton comes out mud-stained. The corporation farms of California and Texas are many times larger than those in the Southeast; the smaller farms have less capital to invest in machinery. The machine works better with some varieties than with others; many growers prefer to have their long-staple cotton hand-picked but use machine strippers for the short sturdy stormproof variety. Hoeing and chopping—thinning out the plants—still demand some hand labor. When there is plenty of cheap labor at hand, it is more economical to hire it than it is to run the machine. As one southeastern grower put it: "As long as I can get cotton picked at $3.00 a hundred pounds—that rate figures to about $6.00 for an eight-hour day—I leave the machine in the shed."

Sweet-potato skins are still too tender for the machine, but those New Jersey growers who use combines for Irish potatoes are reducing their labor needs by a ratio of 33 to 12.

On the horizon and in experimental use are electronic blueberry pickers; fig harvesters; knockers for almonds and olives; tree shakers for cherries and walnuts; planters for celery, tomatoes, and strawberries; onion toppers; and pickle harvesters. The National Pickle Packers Association happily reports a 500 per cent jump in sales in the past twenty-five years; as a nation, we now eat an annual 14 billion pickles (children consuming more than adults do). This phenomenon is of special interest to Michigan, where 23,000 acres of "pickles" (cucumbers) bring in an annual $5,000,000. The elusive pickle hides itself in a tangle of lateral stems and needs to be spotted by a human eye and groped for by human fingers. Michigan State University has two teams of scientists exploring the pickle problem: one to wrestle with a design for a mechanical harvester, the other to restyle the cucumber plant. Hopefully they are co-ordinating their activities to avoid duplicating the bean fiasco.

So far nobody has come up with a strawberry picker, but one could be devised, the experts say. The catch would be its expense; it would necessarily be so delicate and costly a contrivance that it would price strawberries right out of the market.

But machines are on the way and a number are in action. As mechanization takes over their jobs, how long will migrants be necessary? This is a good question, and it raises a corollary: what will become of the migrants?

Paradoxically it is one of the first consequences of mechanization to create in some crops a demand, not for fewer, but for greater numbers of migrants. Automation pushes industrial farming toward crop specialization. Larger land units go under cultivation. But in partially mechanized crops like sugar beets, where monogerm seed and chemical weed control eliminate part but not all of the need for hand labor, the seasonality of migrancy becomes aggravated. Greater and greater numbers of people are needed for shorter and shorter specified—and separated—periods of time. Either more people have to move more often to find work or they have to wait out longer intervals of idleness.

Predictions about seasonal labor needs in agriculture must weigh not only the practicability and the cost of mechanization but a variety of interacting influences: trends in size of farms, in crop specialization, in yields per acre; the availability, the efficient utilization, and the cost of labor; changes in the employment outlook in migrant home-base situations; changes in the industrial employment index; increase in the national population; fashions in consumer tastes for food and textiles; changes in per capita food expenditure; the ratio between income from land if it is farmed and its cash value if it were sold for housing or industrial development.

Projections regarding both population increase and trends in farming have a good deal to say about seasonal farm-labor needs. 1975 predictions picture a national population a third again as large as the 1951–53 average; that is, about 210 million. People will be eating fewer cereals and potatoes, less flour and fats and oils, more frozen fruits and vegetables. The amount of food each person consumes is likely to increase about 10 per cent, chiefly on the theory that because processed foods are easy to prepare, people eat more. If this is true, then the domestic demand for farm products will increase even faster than the population. The extra food will come less from an increase in the number of acres cultivated than it will from more food produced on each acre. Within a recent fifteen-year period combined per acre yield of eighteen leading field crops has increased 40 per cent; within a single year—from 1954 to 1955—7 per cent more cotton was harvested from 12 per cent fewer acres. There must be a point of diminishing returns, but it has yet to be reached. Improvements in transportation and refrigeration now make it possible to use the land best suited to each crop, no matter how isolated its location from the ultimate consumer. Irrigation by plastic or aluminum segmented pipe licks the drought problem, not only in reclaimed deserts in the Southwest but also in a fertile region like southeastern Pennsylvania, where rain is usually plentiful but does not always fall on schedule to quench the thirst of a particular crop.

Since 1940 the actual number of farms in the country has declined by about two million, but this does not necessarily mean less land is under cultivation. As farms grow fewer they grow larger. In 1958 there were one fifth fewer farms than there had been ten years earlier; yet the number of farms containing a thousand or more acres had increased by a third. In 1954 the average farm in the thousand-acre-plus category had 4000 acres, and the trend is moving up. Today the sale of a farm does not mean merely that one grower transfers ownership to another;

two fifths of all farm land sold is bought by established growers or corporations to increase the size of their operation. By 1975 farms will be fewer and larger; they will be more mechanized and more specialized.

Taking everything into account—assuming no wartime emergency, no drastic changes in the national economy, and no spectacular technological advances beyond presently known data —government research specialists were willing, in the late fifties, to forecast a consistent demand for seasonal agricultural labor for each year up to 1975. Now opinion is not so confident; informal affirmations are made with a shade more diffidence. The tempo of crop mechanization seems to be speeding up. Some growers are saying privately that the handwriting is on the wall; the good old days of cheap farm labor are numbered. The era will not depart without a last-ditch fight, but its doom is sealed. Reform legislation for domestic labor and the threat of a cutoff of foreign labor are forcing mechanization. Speaking to the controversy over Mexican importation and Public Law 78, a Farm Bureau leader put it this way: "We want one more extension; after that, mechanization may have made the bracero program unnecessary."

In spite of the classic exemption of farm workers from "Labor," trade unionism in modern American agriculture does have a history, manifested most dramatically in the years from 1930 to 1939.

Although the unpicturesque word "agribusiness" was not to find its way into the language for a couple of decades, the lush twenties saw continuing transformation in the agricultural pattern from family farm to business enterprise. Variously named grower associations, labor exchanges, and labor bureaus were formed and consolidated their strength. Stimulated by state and county agricultural agents, they were eliminating local competition for labor among individual employers and they were attempting, often successfully, to stabilize low wage rates throughout a crop area. By removing the element of personal relationship they were widening the cleavage between employer and worker and tacitly inviting farm labor to move toward collective action.

In contrast to this developing power bloc, the difficulties inherent in orderly organization of migrancy were all too plain. How could a continuous, indigenous leadership take root and grow within a heterogeneous group, disfranchised by mobility, beset by poverty, by ethnic and occupational minority status, by ignorance, rootlessness, and chronic desperation? It is not so extraordinary that collective action made little permanent headway in migrancy—the wonder is that it ever was tried at all.

The story of farm-labor organization during the thirties is compounded of frustration and violence. It is a frightening welter of spontaneous strikes, ephemeral unions, interunion strife, and communist fomentation; a confused and bloody montage of terror and outrage and hunger; of clubs, pick handles, blackjacks, tear gas, and guns; of intimidation by extralegal posses, bands of vigilantes, and night riders; of local police power with a vested interest in lining up on the side of the growers. The picture was not lightened by New Deal legislation like NRA (the National Recovery Act) and AAA (the Agricultural Adjustment Administration) that gave relief to industry, to non-farm labor, and to farm owners, but none to farm labor, that gave legal protection to industrial labor to organize, but none to farm labor. The prevailing traditional view that farm workers were a favored group sheltered and cared for by their employers generated public sympathy for the growers.

The annals of the thirties record 275 separate and identifiable strikes in agriculture. Nearly a quarter of them, sixty-one, broke out within a single year—1933—but no year of the decade was exempt:

Year	Number of Strikes in Agriculture
1930	8
1931	5
1932	10
1933	61
1934	38
1935	30
1936	33
1937	32
1938	35
1939	23
Total	275

More than half of the strikes—140—erupted in California, but twenty-seven other states experienced a share:

Agricultural Labor Strikes
by States
1930–1939

California	140	Missouri	4
Oregon	17	Alabama	3
Ohio	11	Idaho	3
Florida	9	Michigan	2
Washington	9	Minnesota	2
Massachusetts	8	Wisconsin	2
New York	8	Wyoming	2
Connecticut	7	Indiana	1
New Jersey	7	Maryland	1
Arkansas	6	Montana	1
Arizona	6	North Carolina	1
Pennsylvania	6	Vermont	1
Texas	6	Virginia	1
Colorado	5	District of Columbia	1
Illinois	5		

Total   275

Many strikes were marked by complete frustration for the strikers. Yet there were instances in which pay rises resulted. In Santa Clara County, for example, at Mountain View—where in 1960 the California public health task force found little E.C. in his substandard tent dwelling, moderately dehydrated and suffering from pneumococcal meningitis—a cherry pickers' strike in 1933 won a compromise wage settlement of 30¢ an hour. Among the workers in packing sheds and canneries some enduring headway was made, but among the field hands there was little that lasted.

Two exceptions are worthy of note.

One agricultural union enjoyed a tenuous but tenacious survival. It began in 1934 when eighteen sharecroppers, eleven white and eight Negro, met in an abandoned schoolhouse on an Arkansas plantation. Calling itself the Southern Tenant Farmers Union, its early stormy years saw displaced tenant farmers and sharecroppers shift first to day labor and then, as a last resort and a dubious refuge, to migrancy. In 1946 it affiliated with the AFL as the National Agricultural Workers Union and became in 1959 the nucleus for the union drive in the Sacramento Valley in California. In the fall of 1960 it became a division of the Amalgamated Meat Cutters and Butcher Workmen, AFL-CIO, and set up offices in Memphis, looking toward a new organizing drive in the South.

The second notable exception was the successful organization in 1941 of Seabrook Farms in Bridgeton, New Jersey, a setup regarded today with uniform satisfaction by both labor and management. Each gives the other credit for good working relations. According to union leader Leon B. Schachter, success in the Seabrook situation came about because "the Seabrook family . . . was not medieval. It did not meet Local 56's organizing drive with a blind and frenzied counterattack . . . The Seabrooks were then, as they are today, an enlightened management." On the part of the company, the Seabrooks declare that the union grievance procedure is more realistic and more workable than an elaborate personnel structure or a company union, but that basically the relationship works because of the responsible character of the union leadership.

Practically overnight World War II created a radical change in the farm-labor picture. The armed forces and the high employment in defense industries siphoned off the rural labor surplus. Organized agriculture and organized labor found themselves unexpectedly working to the same end: mobilization of all resources in the interests of the war effort. In California both the Associated Farmers and the CIO State Industrial Union Council appealed to the federal government to import Mexican workers as an emergency measure.

From the close of World War II in 1945 until the end of the nineteen fifties organized labor generally limited itself to a prophetic role in behalf of farm labor. AFL-CIO spokesmen testified at hearings and worked with other interested groups to create public awareness of the degree to which farm labor was excluded and exploited. They bore down heavily on the problem of the labor surplus created by the mushrooming of Mexican importation under Public Law 78. The AFL-CIO's 1955 convention unanimously adopted a statement attacking "the loose certification of an alleged 'need' for foreign workers"; called upon Congress to require employers "to offer terms and conditions of employment to United States workers at least comparable to the higher standards they must now offer braceros"; and demanded legislation "to regulate labor contractors, establish regulations for safe transportation, provide better housing and health facilities, and insure educational opportunity for migrant children."

In 1959, on the theory that in the end it is the field workers themselves who must band together to improve their own working conditions, AFL-CIO went to work in earnest to unionize agricultural workers. Their Executive Council assessed the unions one cent a month per member to provide funds, "which, among other matters of importance, will be used to institute large-scale organizing campaigns, particularly with respect to agricultural workers throughout the country."

"The Agricultural Workers Organizing Committee" chose as its first target the state of California, with its 90,000 farms, its $2,500,000,000 agricultural industry, and its heavy dependence on bracero labor. The AWOC spent several months in research and analysis of the situation. It conducted a drive for membership in the National Agricultural Workers Union, defining the benefit to be derived as the negotiation of contracts with growers and growers' associations, contracts that would establish a wage floor at a living level, guarantee greater continuity of employment, and recognize the union for purposes of collective bargaining. It recruited a small staff directly from the fields. It assembled a crew and in the summer of 1959 harvested the crops of Frederick S. Van Dyke. Mr. Van Dyke, mentioned earlier as a more than ordinarily individualistic farmer, paid the workers $1.25 an hour plus a bonus for completion of the field; circulated an open letter, "To My Fellow Farmers," giving his reasons for supporting the unionization of agricultural labor; and testified against Public Law 78 at the congressional hearings in March 1960.

The major burden of Mr. Van Dyke's appeal to farmers was not sentimental. It was based on the self-interest of "every working farmer." He cited the indirect social and tax costs to the community rising from disorganization in the labor market, relief programs, slum conditions, educational retardation, broken families, police problems. He pointed out the gain to the economy of the community if farm wages were spent locally by domestic labor instead of going to Mexico. He added that higher wages based on ability and training and paid according to no-strike contracts would stabilize the labor market and eliminate the farmer's number-one headache. He suggested that unionization of farm labor would have the revolutionary and desirable effect of prodding independent farmers—in contrast to "the large farming syndicates"—to organize in their own behalf to receive higher prices for their products.

In November 1959 AWOC announced in its newsletter that a farm organization called "The Diversified Growers" was building a war chest to fight the union, by calling on members for an assessment of ten cents per acre and up to a thousand dollars per grower.

The summer of 1960 saw the issue joined in earnest.

In the early asparagus crop, which was ordinarily harvested by some 6000 braceros and 1500 domestic workers, the union placed 3200 domestic workers without undue incident.

Cherries were another story.

Mexico will not allow her braceros to work in a situation where there is a labor dispute. Under orders from the United States Department of Labor, the California Farm Placement Service refused to allow braceros to be sent to—or to recruit domestic workers for—farms where AWOC had set up picket lines. One cherry grower estimated his resulting loss at $200,000.

Sixteen California farm organizations set up a Farmers Food Emergency Committee to see that crops were harvested whether labor disputes existed or not. In June the committee sent a delegation of five growers and five lawyers to Washington to get from Secretary of Labor Mitchell "a satisfactory definition of a labor dispute." The growers insisted that the definition in use by the state of California "was lifted right out of the Taft-Hartley Act, which exempts agriculture."

The Labor Department stood firm; but in July, Secretary Mitchell paid tribute to his adversaries. Speaking to the American Federation of Television and Radio Artists, he identified the toughest pressure group he had ever encountered as—not Jimmy Hoffa's Teamsters, not Big Steel, not Republican job-seekers—but "big commercial farm groups, every time legislation is introduced that would stop the importation of migrant farm workers from foreign countries."

In August, Federal Judge Sherrill Holbert denied a petition that he order the U. S. Labor Department to send Mexican farm labor to orchards picketed by domestic workers.

In September the union was counting seventeen strikes in progress and announcing that the bulk of the crops being harvested were coming in under the union scale. The tomato picker was demonstrated at Walnut Grove.

In November union spokesmen were asserting with confidence that they had demonstrated that migratory farm laborers could be organized; that wages in nine San Joaquin Valley counties had been raised some 15 per cent; that the collective-bargaining process had brought a degree of order into the domestic labor market and reduced the number of braceros. Specifically the union took credit for raising the tomato-picking rate from 12¢ to 17¢ a box; the cherry rate from 85¢ to $1.10 for a sixteen-quart bucket. Hourly rates ranged from $1.10 to $1.25.

The bloody violence of 1933 was absent from the 1960 struggle. The AWOC reported "some pressures exerted on growers who participated in collective bargaining," but in the main the weapons were injunctions and legal actions; the arena was the courtroom.

The battle lines were drawn between the organized farm bloc and the California courts on one side and on the other the United States Department of Labor, represented in California by State Farm Placement Director Irving H. Perluss. An added touch of drama was lent to the California situation by the fact that a predecessor of Mr. Perluss, Edward F. Hayes, had left his government post and become general manager of the Imperial Valley Farmers Association.

Mr. Perluss explained to California state legislators his reasons for appealing a Yuba County Superior Court ruling in a case involving the Di Giorgio Fruit Company.

"Growers have strenuously argued that I should have accepted the Superior Court's decision as conclusive and issued state-wide instructions to our staff to ignore the provision in the Secretary of Labor's regulation. The Secretary of Labor has ruled that my office cannot refer workers to any ranch involved in a labor dispute. In the Di Giorgio case the court issued a temporary restraining order ordering the department to resume referrals. I cannot accept the view of the court, either as a lawyer or as an administrator."

In December the National Council of Churches reaffirmed its policy enunciated at intervals since 1951 by urging:

. . . the continuation of current efforts at responsible and democratic labor organization among these [migrant farm] workers. We favor extending to them by law the right of collective bargaining and access to the services of the National Labor Relations Board on a par with other wage workers in industry. We call upon employers of Christian conscience to encourage and stand with these workers in their efforts to gain human dignity, self-respect, and economic security through the well-tested device of union organization.

In its issue of January 21, 1961, the biweekly *California Farmer* deplored "the way church organizations have been drawn into the battle." "Churches are Being Duped" ran the heading of the lead editorial, and it continued: "The union draws the church into the affair by painting a pitiful picture of an enslaved class of people suffering tremendous oppression. The church is naturally sensitive to this type of project and they enter the fray with great enthusiasm. Unfortunately, the church does not make their own impartial study of the situation. You are readily led to this conclusion, because all their pronouncements are word-for-word mouthings of the union propaganda." Apparently previous policy pronouncements of the National Council of Churches had failed to reach the eyes of the *California Farmer*.

In February the scene shifted from the San Joaquin Valley to

Imperial Valley lettuce around El Centro, which is two hundred miles southeast of Los Angeles and a twelve-mile run from the Mexican border. Here the Imperial Valley Farmers Association, representing some 2000 growers of lettuce, carrots, and melons, had contracted for 9400 braceros. The Mexican Consul at Calexico, on mandate from his embassy in Washington, ordered 2000 braceros evacuated from fifteen strike-bound ranches. According to Labor Department ruling, the strikes were legal, but the number of braceros to be evacuated was reduced to 600. Twelve union leaders were arrested on charges of unlawful assembly. A superior court in El Centro granted an injunction to the growers forbidding union picketing at two ranches and ruling that braceros could be used. One report said "some scuffling but no violence"; another that thirty-six men were arrested on assault charges and two Mexicans slightly injured. A twenty-car caravan carrying 120 farmers set out from San Francisco for a show of strength in the Imperial Valley and 600 growers and sympathizers were deputized by the sheriff to maintain order.

There are at least two other angles to the bracero story.

First, even if Public Law 78 were terminated immediately and permanently, there is another way for Mexican farm workers to come into the country. Public Law 414 provides that "an alien having a residence in a foreign country which he has no intention of abandoning" may be admitted to the United States temporarily to perform specified labor. Conditions of admission include certification that "unemployed persons capable of performing such services or labor cannot be found in this country," plus an employer's petition approved by the Attorney General. This is the statute under which temporary workers are imported from the British West Indies, Canada, and Japan, household help from Scandinavia, etc. It applies equally to Mexicans, has been so used, and could be inflated into another Public Law 78.

Second, the bracero situation has crucial bearing on the whole question of relations between the United States and Mexico and indeed between the United States and all of Latin America. There are Central and South American countries that would look with favor upon an opportunity to relieve poverty and unemployment at home by exporting labor to the United States; by them, termination of the Mexican bracero program, unless it were accompanied by a well-conceived, well-administered, well-interpreted program of technical assistance for all of Latin America, could be read as a repudiation of good neighborliness.

The organized farm groups do not all see eye to eye. The California State Grange would like the state to set up an arbitration commission to settle disputes between growers and unions and avoid strikes at harvest periods, even though such a step would mean swallowing the bitter pill of union recognition. The California Farm Bureau believes the government should stay out of the picture, that growers should be allowed to work voluntarily toward solution of their labor problems. Curiously this Farm Bureau stand against government intervention does not hold up when the shoe is on the other foot; the Farm Bureau welcomes government subsidy of labor importation.

It is the large agricultural interests that the union wants to bring to terms, the corporation farms that have gone into "vertical integration," by which the same management makes contracts with small growers for their crops on terms dictated by the company; owns the canning, the freezing, the processing plants; and controls the marketing operations. The Di Giorgio Fruit Company, for example, whose case was cited by Irving Perluss, is incorporated in Delaware; has 400 preferred and 4300 common stockholders; employs 4000 people; engages in the production, harvesting, and marketing of agricultural products; owns 25,000 acres of seasonal crops in California and Oregon and leases additional acreage; owns two wineries and a 13,000,000-gallon bottling plant; owns and operates a lumber mill and a box factory in Oregon (Klamath Lumber and Box Company). Wholly owned subsidiaries are the Di Giorgio Wine Company, the Santa Fe Wine Company, the Padre Vineyard Company, the Earl Fruit Company, Tree Sweet Products Company, S & W Fine Foods Company (99 per cent), and the Philadelphia Terminals Auction Company (98 per cent). Partially owned affiliates are the New York Fruit Auction Corporation (45 per cent) and the Fruit Auction Sales Company (14 per cent).

The large corporations have the independent grower caught in a squeeze. It is not within his power to pass on increased labor costs to the consumer. If he does not contract in advance to sell his crop on company terms, he runs a good chance of finding himself with no market at all for his perishable harvest. If small growers were to allocate time and money to organize themselves in order to bargain with canners, packers, freezers, wholesalers, and chain stores, they would be at least heading toward the point where they could demand prices that would enable them to apply reasonable working and living standards to their own labor.

Interesting problems faced the new Secretary of Labor and the new Secretary of Agriculture when they took office in 1961.

17. HOPE FOR
MIGRANT WORKERS

The brightest hope for the welfare of seasonal
agricultural workers lies with the elimination of
the jobs upon which they now depend, and the
development of programs for the transfer of
workers from agricultural to industrial labor markets. The role of government might then be one
which it could play with dignity. . . . Obviously,
in the meantime, wherever opportunities for im-
provement present themselves, they should be
seized. Whatever the limits of tolerance for reform, they should be exploited to the full. Sec-
ular processes take a long time.
—*Lloyd H. Fisher.*

The controversy over Public Law 78 is one symbol of
panic mentality in industrialized agriculture.

Resistance to housing, sanitation, and transportation regulations is another.

Fear of regulated wage rates is another.

Anti-union mind set is another. Industrialized agriculture has
not been able to bring itself to accept the concept of collective
bargaining as a fact of the modern American economy.

Agriculture still regards itself as different and therefore ex-
cused from responsibility to its workers.

With the argument that vulnerability at harvesttime makes it unique, agriculture successfully hoodwinked supporters of reform legislation in the nineteen thirties and kept itself excluded from the Fair Labor Standards Act and the jurisdiction of the National Labor Relations Board.

Agriculture thereby acquired tacit legal sanction to enjoy unique privileges in its labor practices.

Agriculture retained this exemption to the point where, while industry had to compete for labor by offering terms of employment attractive to American workers, the personnel manager of a factory in the field could secure specified numbers of braceros from a Farm Placement Office subsidized by the federal government.

Historically the Department of Agriculture has fostered the philosophy that agriculture should be exempt. Its wrestlings with the farm problem have never taken farm labor into account. Price supports—with the sole exception of the Sugar Act—acreage controls, soil banks, all the attempts to ease the farm problem leave farm labor completely out of consideration. Book after book—including one by Secretary of Agriculture Ezra Taft Benson—interprets farm policy and offers remedial measures without a mention of responsibility to farm labor. And the attitude seems to be bipartisan. Asked by Dave Garroway on the "Today" show if he was thinking in terms of a minimum wage for agriculture, Secretary of Agriculture Orville Freeman replied substantially in these words: "I do conceive of a fair parity price for the farmer. The minimum wage concept is not a valid comparison. It is a fundamental error to compare the economics of industry with the economics of agriculture."

Today agriculture's right to exemption from labor standards is being for the first time formidably threatened. One challenger is the United States Department of Labor; another is a unit of organized labor geared for action; a third is a United States Senate subcommittee bent on effecting some legislative reform;

and there is an array of private agencies who are saying again what they have been for decades but are saying now with new hope. Their voices have not been entirely unheard through the years, but the public concern they stimulate comes and goes in cycles. Before the present cycle subsides something may happen; agriculture may find itself no longer exempt.

Organized farm groups reveal a growing sensitivity to the image of themselves as exploiters of cheap labor. John Zuckerman, chairman of the California Farmers Food Emergency Committee, refers to himself and his colleagues as "us despised growers" at the same time that he calls the opposition line-up "hordes of pseudo-socio-agricultural experts." "All too frequently in the last two years," he said in the spring of 1960, "this matter of supplemental farm labor has been the central theme of circuses, and I use the word advisedly, spawned in waves of emotionalism, born in the medium of acrimony and misrepresentation, and nurtured in the climate of hysteria and prejudice. . . . I begin to wonder whether I am the venial, brutal beast pictured by them, or merely an American farmer, attempting to make an honest living and possessing a conscientious regard for the welfare of my fellow human beings."

Spokesmen on both sides have been guilty of overstatement. This is as natural as it is indefensible. It takes shock tactics to generate emotion and to shake public apathy. It takes beating the bushes to find an audience for a constructive account of slow progress; it is easy to find a market for a horror story. It is equally easy for the public to become inured to the presence of persistent and chronic insecurity, vulnerability, discrimination, and poverty . . . for others.

It is encouraging that certain individual growers evince increasing ethical concern about farm-labor conditions. The American Farm Bureau Federation itself recommends to its state units that they give consideration to improving migrant state housing regulations, to extending occupational insurance to farm workers, to enacting transportation standards, to regulating child labor, to assurance that local schools are open to migrant children. These are excellent objectives. Even though state and local opinion everywhere does not accept them, their enunciation by the national body indicates how the climate is changing for the better. But the Farm Bureau has yet to support minimum wage, individual worker contracts, guarantee of minimum employment, and working conditions for domestic labor comparable to those available to foreign labor. The climate is not yet that healthy.

In theory mechanization should be good news for both the growers and the migrants.

Too many of the migrant's problems are inherent in the very fact of his migrancy: his housing, his health, his children's education, his lack of opportunity for social and political participation. If mechanization eliminates the need for him to migrate, this should be good; but if it leaves him stranded on a relief roll in a rural slum, it is not good.

If automation is to benefit the migrant, the way must be paved by sound social and economic planning. The forces of agriculture and labor, public and private, cannot begin too soon to work together to anticipate the consequences of mechanization—the economic consequences and the human consequences. Automation in agriculture means a decreasing demand for stoop labor; it means an increasing number of jobs calling for skills. The potential to fill skilled jobs in agriculture is waiting within the present migrant population. The manpower and the innate abilities are there. Given the necessary training, there is no reason why today's migrants cannot compete in tomorrow's mechanized farm-labor market. But this must not be allowed to happen without the application of higher standards to the jobs involved or without attention to the problem of continuity of employment.

Nor will it happen overnight. Meantime agriculture needs migrant labor and migrant people have their own needs to meet.

Organized labor has some of the answers but not all. It can only hope to bring some order into the chaotic farm-labor market. Minimum wage will help, but it will not bring a doctor to an isolated migrant camp; it will not provide decent and sanitary housing; it will not educate the children; it will not end discrimination; it will not offer an alternative to rootlessness.

For some of these needs legislation, both federal and state, will help, and public support can bring it about. But it is the community, every community that depends on migrant labor, that has before it on its doorstep a special opportunity. Here it is that the will and the skill can be found—as in a few places they have been found—to mobilize resources, to make health services available, to open schoolroom doors, to offer opportunity for recreation, for identification with community life, and most of all to encourage among all residents attitudes of accepting migrants, not as stereotypes, but as people. Here it is that the Fontanezes and the Gradys will feel the difference.

Background Reading and
Sources of Information

THE CITIZEN WORKER

There is no dearth of material about the culture patterns of ethnic groups in the United States. A few books have been specially helpful in supplementing personal acquaintance with migrant people.

Spanish-Speaking Groups in the United States (John H. Burma, Duke University Press, 1954) gives major attention to the social, economic, and cultural problems of Mexican Americans, including migrant farm workers. *Cultural Difference and Medical Care* (Lyle Saunders, Russell Sage Foundation, 1954) is directed to a professional audience, but medical background is not essential to an understanding of its sympathetic presentation of Mexican folkways and its guidance for bridging cultural chasms. The same is true on a smaller scale of the picture of medical problems given in *Health in the Mexican-American Culture* (Margaret Clark, University of California Press, 1959), which focuses on a single community in northern California. Less recent but valuable in perspective is *Latin Americans in Texas* (Pauline R. Kibbe, University of New Mexico Press, 1946).

In *Cultural Values of American Ethnic Groups* (Sister Frances Jerome Woods, Harper, 1956) the author discusses institutional and family intercultural problems from a social-work viewpoint. She draws her illustrations from a variety of ethnic groups, several of whom appear in the migrant stream. About Anglo migrants there is valuable data in a paper by William H. Metzler on *Socio-Economic Aspects of Manpower Adjustments: Low-Income Rural Areas* (Rural

Sociology, Vol. 24, No. 3, September 1959). Among many resources for Indian understanding two books by Ruth Underhill stand out: *Red Man's America* (University of Chicago Press, 1953) and *Here Come the Navaho* (U. S. Bureau of Indian Affairs, 1953). Regarding Puerto Rican migrant workers, the primary source of information is the office in New York City of the Migration Division of the Commonwealth of Puerto Rico. As to numbers of Puerto Rican and Indian people in the migrant population, the U. S. Labor Department Annual Report for 1959 gives a figure of 13,000 contracted Puerto Ricans and estimates an equal number of "walk-ins"; and it reports 45,000 reservation Indians placed in eighteen states in addition to those who apply at employment offices and "need no special services."

They Follow the Sun (Koos, Florida State Board of Health, 1957) describes an exploration of the total life pattern of a Negro crew in the eastern-seaboard migration. The social characteristics and the problems of 200 families are reported in fascinating detail with liberal quotations from the migrants themselves. *Migratory Farm Workers in the Atlantic Coast Stream,* a U. S. Department of Agriculture study in the Belle Glade area of Florida, has an abundance of data on the east-coast migration. A reliable basic resource on Negro groups, including plantation culture, is *The Negro in the United States* (E. Franklin Frazier, Macmillan, rev. ed., 1957).

In 1960 the Bureau of Labor of Oregon published *And Migrant Problems Demand Attention* (Tom Current and Mark Martinez Infante), the final report of two years of studies. Packed with data, it manages at the same time to be highly readable and specially revealing in the delicate domain of attitudes—migrant, grower, and community.

In 1959 the yearbook of the U. S. Department of Labor was issued in the form of a *Farm Labor Fact Book.* Its section on migrant farm workers includes travel patterns, a description of government efforts to match labor supply with demand, and case studies of migrant workers.

State Farm Placement annual reports are excellent sources of regional information, and they have been freely used in this book. The tabulation of domestic and foreign migrants by states in Chapter IV is based on the January 1960 issue of *Farm Labor Market Developments* (U. S. Department of Labor).

Migratory Labor in American Agriculture (1951), the report of the President's Commission, is basic resource for any current migrant-labor study, as are the bulletins of the President's Committee on Migratory Labor, issued periodically as *Migratory Labor Notes*.

THE FOREIGN WORKER

The progression of foreign farm labor through California history during the second half of the nineteenth century and the first half of the twentieth is expertly presented and documented in *The Harvest Labor Market in California* by Lloyd H. Fisher (Harvard University Press, 1953). The events leading to the present importation program from the emergency measures of World War II up to 1950 are reviewed in *Migratory Labor in American Agriculture* (cited earlier). As the wetback invasion moved to a climax, the story in both Texas and California was vividly covered in the New York *Times* from its Los Angeles news bureau by Gladwyn Hill.

An account of the bracero program with emphasis on its abuses is contained in *Strangers in Our Fields* by Ernesto Galarzo, based on a study financed by a grant-in-aid from the Fund for the Republic and published in 1956 by the Joint United States-Mexican Trade Union Committee. This report explains the problems from the bracero's point of view:

All the bracero knows is that he must pay an insurance premium once a week and have as much as a week's pay withheld to guarantee his transportation expenses back to the reception center. The state law that protects him when he is hurt on the job; the obligations of his employer to transport him in safe and reasonably comfortable vehicles; his right to a minimum of hygiene in camp—these rights are largely unknown to him. Not knowing what ground to stand on, he is by turns obsequious, reserved, quietly resentful, or fatalistic.

When the National is in need of counsel or advice, or some immediate personal service, he turns to those around him who speak Spanish and know the lay of the land. The truck driver, the camp caretaker, the field foreman, the bartenders, the small merchants and the taxi drivers are the makeshift counselors and social workers to whom the National looks. Those persons are almost never known other than by their first names. One bracero left several week's wages in the safekeeping of a town bar but did not ask for a receipt because "it seemed ugly to me." Typically he knew nothing else about the transaction except that "it was in Stockton and the bartender's name was Pete."

And the report places on the contractor the major responsibility for the difficulties the bracero encounters:

What the bracero does not know about his rights is not likely to be taught him by the contractors. They and their foremen and their camp managers see themselves as men of parts, able to solve almost any problem—and without reference to the International Agreement or the work contract. They do not hesitate to diagnose illness, to turn down requests for a doctor, to provide or withhold services actually made mandatory by the Agreement or the Work Contract, to change the rate of pay, to select favored individuals or crews for available work, to decide on the kinds and quantity of food the men under their supervision shall be served, to decide whether they will issue an extra blanket or install a heater, to deny or concede transportation to town or to the area association pool in cases of contract termination. Since the contractor is the first person in authority and for the most part the only person with whom the bracero is in an immediate relationship, he becomes interpreter, administrator, and judge—law or no law.

From another point of view, a series of articles by Elmer Kelton, agricultural editor of the *San Angelo* (Texas) *Standard-Times* (reprinted in the House subcommittee hearings for 1958 and again in 1960), based on interviews in villages of northern Mexico, gives a brighter picture of the bracero experience:

Over and over, and over again, we asked former braceros the same question. Were they unhappy while they were on the other side? Were they ever mistreated? Were they ever discriminated against or made to feel inferior?

I actually hoped I would find some who would say yes. It would look like a purposely slanted one-sided report if it didn't contain some adverse comments.

But in a week of visiting and a thousand miles of driving in the

State of Chihuahua, we didn't find a single ex-bracero who showed any resentment or said he had been mistreated.

They liked some employers better than others, to be sure, but they evinced no dislike for any of them.

Dozens of times we heard the words *muy contento*—very content. And *muy buen patrón*—very good boss. . . . There is opposition to the bracero program in Mexico. But it does not come from the braceros themselves. It seems to stem mostly from people who have had no firsthand experience with the program.

According to Rev. James L. Vizzard, S.J., representing the National Catholic Rural Life Conference, the Roman Catholic Church in Mexico does not favor the program because of its destructive effect on family life:

Perhaps the most fundamentally adverse aspect of the Mexican farm labor program is the fact that it requires the absence of hundreds of thousands of men from home and families for many weeks or months and in not a few cases even for years. So disruptive of family life is such a situation that the Mexican hierarchy of the Catholic Church is urging the total elimination of this program.

How much of a lift Public Law 78 gives to the Mexican economy is difficult to determine. Hearsay puts the bracero program as third in sources of national income, with exports first and tourism second. According to a report in the New York *Times* of March 15, 1959, the Bank of Mexico reported that 428,593 Mexican migratory workers had sent home $35,700,000.

The cost to the federal government of Mexican importation runs around $2,000,000. Each employer pays a fee for each bracero for whom he contracts. The federal budget (Combined Statement of Receipts, Expenditures, and Balances of the U. S. Government for the Fiscal Year Ended June 20, 1960) includes two estimated figures:

Compliance Activities Mexican Farm Labor Program	850,000
Salaries and Expenses Mexican Farm Labor Progarm	1,359,773
Total	$2,209,773

The 1959 report on the *Mexican Farm Labor Program* by four consultants to the Secretary of Labor emphasized two deficiencies:

Adverse Effect on Domestic Labor

There are indications of some employer preference for Mexicans over domestic workers because they represent an assured work force of premium adult male labor. . . . The average farm wage worker can only expect to work about 125 days a year at farm jobs. If foreign workers are available, seasons of agricultural employment may be further compressed by using more workers at peak. . . . Knowledge of the availability of Mexican nationals weakens the domestic workers' bargaining position and contributes to the depression of area wage levels . . . in the case of Mexicans used in the machine packing and sorting of vegetables in the field, American packing-house workers have been displaced. However, the displaced workers are not necessarily available to transfer to field jobs because of changes in the job content as well as a lowering of wages and the conditions of employment. Consequently Mexicans are requested for field packing work while higher-paid domestic shed workers are laid off. . . . Under Public Law 78 foreign workers may be used for any commodity or product which the Secretary of Agriculture deems essential. Since the inception of the law, however, the Secretary of Agriculture has not exercised his discretion to declare any commodities nonessential, even those which are in surplus supply and heavily subsidized. More than 70 per cent of all Mexicans are employed at peak work in crops which are in surplus supply . . . some employers of foreign labor make only token efforts to co-operate in obtaining domestic workers . . . domestic workers who are employed at a lower wage prior to the time Mexican workers are recruited do not necessarily receive an increase when higher paid Mexicans arrive on the job.

Determination of Prevailing Wage

The prevailing wage to be paid Mexican workers is determined by conducting surveys at frequent intervals among samples of employers of domestic workers in areas where foreign workers are used. . . . The prevailing wage concept may work satisfactorily in situations where wage rates are determined by competitive forces in the labor market, and there are so few Mexicans that their presence does not upset this equilibrium. Actually, however, the availability of a potential reserve of foreign labor generally influences the wage levels in the area for crops on which Mexicans are usually employed, and on other crops as well . . . wage levels tend to become fixed in areas and activities where Mexicans are employed . . . A special problem is posed within areas in which the farm work force is preponderantly Mexican national. It is generally recognized that prevailing wage determinations are meaningless in such cases. Some of the heavily dominated crops are lettuce, citrus, melons, and carrots in parts of Arizona; tomatoes, lettuce, citrus, strawberries, sugar beets, and melons, citrus fruit, beans, peppers, cucumbers in parts of Texas; cotton in New Mexico; pickles and lettuce in Colorado; and sugar beets in a number of states.

Regarding the guarantee of fifty cents an hour or equivalent of which Armando Santiago was assured in Chapter VI, examination of the contract shows a mention only of "prevailing wage"; no amount is specified. In practice, however, as Newell Brown of the U. S. Labor Department told the House subcommittee: "The Mexican Government informally, but nevertheless rigidly, will not permit a Mexican worker to cross the border for work here for less than fifty cents." The Labor Department Annual Report (1959) cites a new ruling in this connection: "Where the piece rates do not enable 90 per cent of the workers to earn 50¢ an hour, adjustments in rate levels are an employer's responsibility."

English translations of the bracero contract and of the guide given to Armando Santiago appear in the *Farm Labor Fact Book* (cited earlier). This book contains also a case history of a bracero's typical experience.

The figures in the tabulation of "Braceros Imported Under Contract" and "Wetbacks Returned to Mexico" are derived from reports of the U. S. Departments of Agriculture and Labor and from the Immigration and Naturalization Service.

The rumored compromise between the Secretary of Agriculture and the Secretary of Labor is described in a special dispatch to the New York *Times* from its Washington correspondent, Joseph A. Loftus, dated March 30, 1960:

The administration has decided not to support farm labor legislation this year. The effect of the decision is to block proposals to end the program of importing Mexican labor, aid domestic migrants, and establish a minimum wage. A House agricultural subcommittee will be formally advised of the decision tomorrow. . . .

An agreement between Ezra Taft Benson, Secretary of Agriculture, and James P. Mitchell, Secretary of Labor, was worked out at the White House, reportedly under the direction of Robert E. Merriam, deputy assistant to the President for interdepartmental affairs. It has the appearance of a compromise, in which both Secretaries backed off in their demands temporarily. Organized labor and liberal spokesmen, however, have indicated they suspect the demands of Mr. Benson and agricultural interests in Congress were made for bargaining purposes. These groups believe the compromise is a victory for growers and the Farm Bureau Federation.

The growers have a voice on the White House staff. Jack Z. Anderson, former Republican representative from California and a pear grower, is administrative assistant to the President for Congressional liaison.

The direct quotations in Chapter VII appear in the hearings before the subcommittee on Equipment, Supplies and Manpower of the House Committee on Agriculture, March 22–31, 1960.

LIFE ON THE SEASON

For understanding the setting and the circumstances of migratory living and the role of legislation in alleviating its problems, four pamphlets contain important background data. Two of these were issued in 1959 by the National Advisory Committee on Farm Labor: *Report on Farm Labor* and *The Position of Farm Workers in Federal and State Legislation* (Robin Myers). *The Migrant Farm Worker in America* (Pollitt and Levine) was prepared for the Subcommittee on Migratory Labor of the U. S. Senate Committee on Labor and Public Welfare (1960). *Report to the President on Domestic Migratory Farm Labor* (1960) summarizes the work of the President's Committee and the present situation.

Housing

The most illuminating existing study of migrant housing was made at the request of the President's Committee (Mirengoff and Shostack, U. S. Dept. of Labor and Florida Industrial Commission, 1958): *Housing for Florida's Migrants: A Survey of Migratory Farm Labor Housing in Dade County*. It gives a comprehensive report on the housing of 1300 families and 5600 single workers at the peak of a winter crop season. Most of the people were living in one or another of seventy-one labor camps; the rest occupied rented quarters in small communities. Of special interest is the information on worker attitudes toward housing and the figures on costs of camp construction and maintenance.

The report notes that living conditions "are discussed all too frequently in a highly charged emotional setting," and it bends backward to be objective. It records the fact that "some camp operators told the survey team that the migrants did not mind crowding, did not want flush toilets, and even preferred rowdy, loose social environments." When the migrants themselves were asked what they did and did not like about their housing, they were often reluctant to express themselves; it seems reasonable to assume that they feared their replies might in some way be used against them. Those who did comment favorably mentioned space and privacy, solid construction, and good camp supervision and policing. Those who mentioned drawbacks cited dilapidation, overcrowding, lack of privacy, inadequate toilet, bathing, and cooking facilities, lack of schools for the children, and lack of camp supervision and policing. The repetition of "policing" in the migrant replies led the writers to comment that few camps appeared to provide the type of regulation the people had in mind.

Initial costs for camp construction ranged from $7500 for the average small camp (housing up to fifty people) to $115,000 for an average large camp (housing several hundred; the largest in the survey had a population of 2000). Where rent was charged the going rate was $3.75 per week per family. Most growers, however, found it an advantage to charge no rent. "The camps assured them of a work force during periods of strong competition for the area's labor supply. All of the camp operators interviewed indicated that provision of housing made it easier to obtain and retain migrant labor."

Federal legislation presently proposed calls for insured housing loans to growers, to non-profit groups, and to migrants themselves.

Transportation

The account of the journey of a crew from Florida to Virginia (Chapter XI) comes from *They Follow the Sun* (Koos, already cited).

There is no common pattern for transportation charges. Some crew leaders make a charge and take it out of subsequent earnings; some make no charge. The U. S. Department of Labor Annual Report (1959) states that some employers advance transportation at the rate of one cent a mile per worker; that this is generally withheld from wages, sometimes being refunded as a bonus when the workers remain to finish the job.

Social Security

In spite of difficulties in making social security fit migrant patterns, the program is working in at least one notable case.

To celebrate its twenty-fifth birthday, the Old-Age and Survivors' Insurance Bureau collected data on those of its beneficiaries who had passed the century mark; it found 130. Nine of them were still gainfully employed, and the dean of these nine was a 118-year-old ex-migrant. Charlie Smith's vocation as a seasonal farm worker did not make him eligible for social security until 1956; he was then 114. Even after his benefits began coming in he kept on picking fruit for a couple of years, and then, at the age of 116, he opened his own hot-dog stand in Polk City, Florida. His memories of life and labor go back a long time. When he was twelve he was captured by slave traders off the coast of Liberia, and a year later, in 1855, he was sold on the auction block in New Orleans, on the Fourth of July.

The grower's adverse comment on social security for migrant workers (quoted in Chapter XI) comes from the Koos study (already cited).

Crew Leaders

There is little documented information available on the "responsible" crew leader, but it is generally acknowledged that "Cap Jackson" in Chapter IX is a prototype of many who perform countless services for their people and see them through all kinds of difficulties. (The crew leaders whose families travel with them appear to be more dependable than those who go it alone.)

On the other hand, the Oregon study (already cited) found "more than isolated instances" of a long list of types of exploitation engaged in by crew leaders and contractors. It cites illustrations of various practices:

A grocery-store operator on the highway near one camp certified to us that he had been propositioned in the manner which is often quite successful for the contractor. The contractor came to him and said substantially: "You are getting my people's trade in here. I estimate they spend here some $1000 per week. I figure I ought to get something of this; I take 25 per cent and you jack up the prices. They will keep on buying here and I see to it. If you do not agree, I take the trade somewhere else." The reason we cite this example is that in this case the grocer did not agree. He lost 90 per cent of the migrant trade.

A contractor in this area operates what would be a pawn shop if it were located on a downtown street, which it is not. The migrants (from several different crews) pawn their valuables to him and he lends them money. His fees for services are as high as $10 a week on a loan of $20, depending to some extent upon whether he figures he can control the borrower through the borrower's contractor. The low fee is about $5 per week on a $20 loan. He moves an estimated $2000 monthly on this one side line alone.

Another case illustrates the occasional association of the farmer in the schemes of the contractor. A contractor brought in twenty-six workers from across the border in Texas. They were all in possession of conditional immigration permits. Upon their arrival at a certain farm, the farmer took their papers away to guarantee that the workers would remain with him the entire season. The housing, sanitary, and working conditions were hard to believe until personal investigation verified them.

The state and federal tax men were very interested in our findings, too, and one of these agencies sent men into the field with us to see at firsthand what was going on. They found relatively few of the contractors who had ever filed either a personal income-tax return or a withholding declaration. They probably would have found the same to be true of the migrants if they had checked them.

Earnings

The information about earnings of Texas migrants is contained in *Incomes of Migratory Agricultural Workers* (Metzler and Sargent, U. S. Department of Agriculture and Texas Agriculture Experiment Station, 1960). The 1300 workers in the 450 households surveyed averaged an annual 131 days of work and annual earnings of $780.

The monumental two-volume study of *Problems Involved in Applying a Federal Minimum Wage to Agricultural Workers* (Harry S. Kantor, U. S. Department of Labor, 1960) goes thoroughly into the complexities of wage regulation in agriculture: the peculiar nature of agricultural production; piece-rate picking and its parallel in the needle trades; the variety of perquisites sometimes furnished by employers; the chaos inherent in the migratory labor market; standards for minors; premiums for overtime; the effect of a minimum wage on productivity and on prices. In conclusion the author states:

The minimum wage needs to be set with due regard for the capacity of agriculture to adjust to it . . . On this basis, the merits of a minimum wage for farm workers can be considered in terms of its potentialities for inducing improvements in productivity, reshaping the structure of the farm work force and labor market, rationalizing the use of labor, and improving the earning power and income of those who depend upon farm wages for a living—according to some standard consistent with technological possibilities in agriculture and consonant with expectations of American life.

Day Haul

Where large farms are located near urban centers like Philadelphia, Baltimore, Oakland (California), Portland (Oregon), the day haul is widely used. The Bureau of Employment Security estimates 300,000 workers recruited in this way. The sequence of the

Philadelphia crew leaders in *First Interlude* is based on the record of Senator Harrison Williams' subcommittee hearings.

A Palm Beach County health Report (*Migrant Project* 1959) describes the day-haul picture in Belle Glade:

In downtown Belle Glade there is an area known as the "loading zone" where the migrant laborers gather each morning between the hours of six and seven. Labor trucks surround the loading zone, and the laborers mill from truck to truck listening to the driver quote the prices to be paid for picking vegetables. At seven o'clock, a loud whistle sounds; the migrants scatter to the trucks they have chosen, and they leave for the day, returning from the fields in late afternoon.

Health

There are two excellent sources of information on migrant health problems and some attempts to reduce them: *Migrant Project* 1959, describing the Palm Beach County experiment mentioned in Chapter XIII; and *Health Conditions and Services for Domestic Seasonal Agricultural Workers and Their Families in California* (California Department of Public Health, 1960). In addition, a number of the illustrations used in Chapter XIII are drawn from *Migratory Labor Notes* (cited earlier; November 1960 issue).

The California report recommends that state funds be made available to those counties desiring to develop field clinics locally staffed; to provide extra nurses in order to extend to migrant people the existing treatment facilities; to allow migrants to use hospital beds at county expense; to provide transportation to clinics; to improve sanitation in housing and in fields. Further, the recommendations urge abolition of county hospital residence requirements and exploration into prepaid health plans for migrant workers similar to those required by law for foreign workers.

The "Florida sores" mentioned in Chapter XIII are found chiefly on children who have been playing in fields of muck-grown vegetables. The muck burns the skin, and the sores fester. Their acquisition is most common in Florida, but it does occur wherever migrant families work in muck, as in the drained sections of the Montezuma marshes in central New York.

Regarding the incidence of mental disturbance among migrants, one public-health nurse has found more disturbed people among single workers than in families. Howard University is now conducting a study on the mental health of migratory people.

Welfare

The description of the 1958 Florida freeze in Chapter IX is based on an editorial in the March 1958 issue of the *National Council Outlook*. Almost every winter a disaster similar to this one hits migrant workers somewhere in the country. In 1959 the scene was Nevada, and the enemy was not weather but a boll weevil invasion of the Arizona cotton fields that sent upward of a thousand people in family groups to the Moapa Valley, sixty-five miles northeast of Las Vegas, a month before the radishes, onions, and tomatoes were ready for harvest. The governor of Nevada declared a state of emergency; the Roman Catholic Church of Las Vegas collected food and clothing; tents were trucked in from the Nellis Air Force Base.

The experience of New York State in meeting welfare problems without a residence requirement is documented in *The Movement of Population and Public Welfare in New York State* (December 1958).

Community Attitudes

In *Second Interlude,* each item is adapted from something that was actually said or done somewhere; most of them ocurred within the personal experience of the author.

By contrast, the Oregon study (already cited) tells of attitude changes stemming in large part from the activity of one police chief, who has:

. . . not only exercised the most constructive law enforcement program in the state, but also exposed community leaders to his own serious concern for the individual migrant. Merchants have responded in their pricing policies. The local theater has developed a program of weekly Spanish-language movies. Farmers have redoubled their efforts to improve living conditions. The churches have launched a vigorous social action program. As often as not, the germ of progress was originally planted by this official. He is well known to the migrant people and he is that rarity—an arm of the law beloved by migrants who traditionally distrust laws and law men. . . . Many of the Spanish-American group do not speak sufficient English to pass a driver's license test, even though they may know the words on highway signs. The result is that driver's license laws are blissfully ignored all over the state. . . . This bliss is sometimes interrupted by a diligent policeman, but the end result is either further offenses or hasty retreat to a state in which the migrant can drive the automobile that is so necessary to his livelihood . . . our subject . . . made arrangements for a Spanish-speaking Motor Vehicle Inspector to give tests. As the program developed, migrants began to come in from all over the western part of the state to this mecca where they could obtain a driver's license. It took some work, some co-operation from interested agencies, some imagination. *It took practically no money. This is not only a typical example of the kind of law enforcement needed; it is also an example of how inexpensively many of the migrant problems can be solved, if given some thought.*

Education

The educational problems of migrant children are set forth definitively by Shirley E. Greene in *The Education of Migrant Children* (National Education Association, 1954). The book is an account of findings in four centers; the Glades area of Palm Beach County, Florida; Northampton County, Virginia; Guadelupe County, Texas; and Vermilion and Iroquois counties, Illinois. *A Study of Migrant Education* by Jerome G. Manis (Western Michigan University, 1958) presents findings from a survey in Van Buren County, Michigan. Southern Illinois is the locale of a study of *The Social Problems of Migrant Farm Laborers: Effect of Migrant Farm Labor on the Education of Children* (Melvin S. Brooks, Southern Illinois University, 1960).

Guidance in methods, techniques, and curricula in dealing with migrant children is found in *Teaching Children Who Move with the Crops* (Fresno County Schools, Fresno, California, 1955);

Working with Migrant Children in our Schools (Florida State Department of Education); and *Learning on the Move* (Colorado State Department of Education, 1960).

The New Jersey experience of "Howard" in Chapter XIV is described in an article in *Survey*, May 1949.

Shifting of Home Bases

The Gradys' happy if precarious landing in the bus camp in a northeastern state is symptomatic of a growing trend in migrancy, although in most cases the results are more precarious than happy.

From widely separated sections of the country comes word that many migrants are ceasing to migrate or at least that they are changing home base from South to North or from East to West. In Suffolk County, Long Island, Negro migrants are staying through the winter instead of returning South. Texas Mexican families are staying on in Ohio, Indiana, Illinois, Michigan. A Farm Placement official estimates that in one Texas community that virtually empties itself every spring 15 per cent of the families do not return.

Nobody has measured the size or persistence of the trend, or the consequences for the migrants, but it is having an impact on the counties in which the settlements are mushrooming. Up and down the length of the San Joaquin Valley in California, migrant refugees from poverty and discrimination in the deep South, in Texas and Arizona, in Arkansas and Oklahoma and Missouri and Kentucky are staked out in rural slums outside of corporation limits, without fire or police protection, water supply, facilities for disposal of garbage or sewage, or any vestige of social regulation or control. There is settlement after settlement of derelict shacks, conglomerations of tar paper, old billboards, and scrap metal. In a paper on *Human Resources and California Agriculture* (1959) the Agricultural Workers Organizing Committee comments that "the farm labor lexicon needs to be enriched to the extent of an appropriate term for this particular element within the farm labor force," and suggests "shoestringers," since the settlements are coming to be known as "shoestring communities." The paper continues: ". . . (the people) are marked by two distinguishing characteristics: they attempt to make a living entirely or largely from agricultural labor; they wish, if possible, to make this living from a single base of operations. That is to say, they have no desire to return to a state of migrancy from which so many of them have only recently escaped."

FRIENDS OF THE HARVESTERS

As indicated in Chapter VII, numerous private agencies work in behalf of migrant people. A number of them co-ordinate their efforts through membership in the National Council of Agricultural Life and Labor in Washington. In 1959 the Catholic Council on Working Life sponsored a national conference in Chicago to consider problems relating to stabilization of migrant farm labor; in 1960 a Roman Catholic Bishops' Committee was formed with headquarters in Chicago to work nationally in the interests of migratory labor.

The development of the Migrant Ministry is recorded in three publications of the National Council of Churches: *Four Decades of the Migrant Ministry; The Migrant Ministry Today;* and *The Fifth Decade.* The issue of Information Service for November 12, 1960 (Vol. xxxix, No. 19), contains additional information.

The files of local newspapers in the thirty-four states in which the Migrant Ministry functions afford the best source of human interest about the grass-roots operation. For example, a feature story in the *Forrest City* (Arkansas) *Gazette* describes a downtown hospitality center for cotton-picking braceros. It reads in part:

If the word spreads around the haciendas of faraway Mexican points that there's a place in Yanqui land called Arkansas where folks are *muy amigable,* much of the credit will be due to what has been done at Forrest City. Business firms, religious and civic groups, and individuals alike have all had a hand in providing Mexican laborers a downtown gathering point on Saturdays. A checking service for personal belongings, clean rest rooms, entertainment, and an abundance of friendly smiles have all served happy and multiple purposes. Better understanding between local citizens and the Mexican nationals has been achieved. There has been almost complete elimination of incidents which in times past brought the workmen into trouble with the law. Since the Center opened a year ago in September, there has been only one arrest and that was for an offense outside the city. The Fiesta Night that climaxed this year's activities found more than a hundred Mexicans at the Center and a goodly crowd of local people, including Mayor Rogers Deadrick, Chief of Police George Trusty, and Farm Placement Chief Joe B. Posey, who grew up along the Texas Mexican border and served as interpreter for the speakers. The language difficulty in informal conversation was overcome to some extent by the efforts—some words and much gesturing—on the part of guests and hosts alike. Punch and cakes liberally dispensed brought considerable expression of *muchas gracias*. Next year? Going to open the Center again, come cotton-picking time.

The feature is illustrated with a picture of Pablo Lopez Jimenez, bracero from the state of Aguascalientes, proudly displaying a water color of a cactus, for which he won first prize in an art contest at the Forrest City *Centro Mexicano*.

FUTURE OF THE HARVESTERS

Mechanization

The information on mechanization in agriculture comes from a variety of sources: personal observation in the field, interviews with growers, magazine articles and press reports, and publications of the Department of Agriculture and the Farm Placement Service.

Numbers and Sizes of Farms

The preliminary findings of the 1959 Census of Agriculture (issued in January 1961) report 3,700,000 farms. This is the smallest number since 1870; it represents a 23 per cent decline since 1954. The number of farms raising vegetables for sale declined 35 per cent. At the same time acreage decreased only 3 per cent, and average farm size climbed from 242 acres in 1954 to 302 in 1959. In 1925 there were 63,000 farms of over a thousand acres; by 1959 the number had more than doubled itself to reach 136,000, and 800,000 farm operators were leasing additional acreage. Specialization increased faster betwen 1954 and 1959 than at any time in our national history.

The Squeeze on the Small Farmer

Data on the changing structure of agriculture are summarized in Agricultural Information Bulletin No. 215: *Keeping Abreast of Change in the Rural Community.* This bulletin gives some interesting figures on increased marketing costs; they shed light on the squeeze in which the small farmer finds himself. In 1957 farmers produced 11 per cent more food and received $700,000,000 less cash than they did in 1951. In contrast, consumers paid food processors and marketing middlemen $7,400,000,000 more in 1957 than they did in 1951, and corporate profits in the food industry increased by $700,000,000. In other words, the farmers' take dropped in the same amount that corporate profits increased.

In this connection the Oregon study (cited earlier) states: "At first hand, we watched a major employee of the processor tell off a grower. The grower had asked for some idea of what the price would be on the fruit he was delivering and was curtly informed that if he didn't like the setup, he could take his produce home, there being no other practical way to dispose of his crop."

The family farmer who employs little or no outside help is beginning to realize that low wages for the migrant-labor army have a depressing effect on the value of his own labor. Commenting on the predicament of the small farmer, Newell Brown of the U. S. Labor Department told the Texas Citrus and Vegetable Growers and Shippers Convention in Dallas (September 14, 1959):

. . . those farmers who depend almost entirely on the labor of family members plus some exchange of labor back and forth with neighboring families . . . comprise more than 50 per cent of all farms in the country. These family farmers . . . are being heard from more and more. As one of them wrote to Secretary Mitchell: ". . . the cost of labor on the large farms pretty well determines the value of farm products I have to sell. A 70-hour-plus week at 50 cents an hour is pretty rough competition to beat." As this farmer sees it, holding down the wages of hired labor has the effect of holding down the value of his own labor. When market prices are influenced by large supplies of vegetables grown by hired labor paid 50 cents per hour, can the family farm hope to make a decent living growing market vegetables with its own labor?

Trade Unions in Agriculture

The history of collective action among farm workers in the United States is traced in detail by Stuart Jamieson of the University of British Columbia in *Labor Unionism in American Agriculture* (U. S. Department of Labor, 1945).

An acount of organized labor's relations with the Seabrook Farms in New Jersey appears in the *I. U. D. Digest* (AFL-CIO, Winter 1953), in an article by Leon Shachter, President of Local 56, Amalgamated Meat Cutters and Butcher Workmen of N.A. It is true, Mr. Shachter states, that the contract specifies seasonal wages that are lower than those for year-round labor, and it does not cover piecework. But the contract does provide for a tight curb on lay-offs, a seniority system, and a grievance procedure, and it does protect the workers in their living as well as their working conditions.

There is an interesting angle to the serious injection of organized labor into the migratory structure, and it is this: the trade union threatens the entire crew-leader system. Employers find the crew leader-contractor a convenience, and so do Farm Placement officials. But labor contends that responsible unions would perform the same functions to better advantage for both worker and employer. Lloyd Fisher points this out in *The Harvest Labor Market in California* (already cited):

The trade union and the labor contractor are implicit competitors . . . It is reasonably clear that successful unionization of seasonal workers would either destroy the contract system or transfer its functions to the trade union in which the seasonal workers were organized . . . Obviously the functions that producers assign to contractors they would bitterly resist granting to trade unions. Psychologically, if not legally or technologically, the contractor is regarded by the producer as part of his own management apparatus, and if he chooses to hire these management services from a contractor rather than providing them more directly from within his own enterprise, no precedent is thereby established which would be remotely applicable to a trade union. Yet it is equally clear that the services rendered are important and even necessary services, and it is conceivable that a responsible trade union could perform these functions more efficiently than does the labor contractor at present.

The A.W.O.C. (in a paper on *The Manufactured "Labor Shortage"
and "Crop Loss" of 1959*) makes a less objective comment:

Growers who wail that they cannot pay more than their present
substandard wage rates should tell the whole truth. Californians
might find it very intriguing. Growers are paying from 23¢ to 25¢
a box to have their peaches picked. Of this workers receive slightly
more than half. The rest is pocketed by labor contractors who have
attached themselves to the throats of farm workers. Growers are
not only *able* to pay a living wage for peach picking; they are already paying it. But that part of the wage which would make the
difference between mere existence and meaningful living is being
siphoned off by parasites whose principal contribution to society is
to perpetuate the chaos of the farm-labor market. If growers were
genuinely concerned about a "labor shortage," they could very
easily attract a superabundance of peach pickers by eliminating the
labor contractors entirely, or reducing the size of the bite contractors are presently putting on the workers' wages.

The Farm Placement Subsidy

The amount of federal subsidy for state Farm Placement activities
can only be estimated. The program is a part of the United States
Employment Service, and many of the people responsible for Farm
Placement have other responsibilities as well. The federal budget
for 1960 contained an item of $323,000,000 granted to states for
"unemployment compensation and employment services administration." On a basis of estimated man-years of work devoted to
Farm Placement in the states, the Bureau of Employment Security
estimates 1960 expenditures of $6,335,000 for salaries and pensions
and $3,345,000 for transportation and administration. The sum of
these—$9,680,000—represents the Bureau's figure for the cost to
the federal government of state Farm Placement operations.

The Farm Placement Service is designed to assist both the growers
and the workers. According to the United States Department of
Labor Annual Report for 1959:

The Bureau's Farm Labor Service has the responsibility of guiding
and co-ordinating programs to assist both growers and farm laborers,

including domestic migratory workers and foreign farm labor. Chief function of the operation is to bring together agricultural workers and employers, including those engaged in food processing. However, such diverse but related activities as estimating crop yield to determine manpower requirements, acting in emergencies to avert crop loss, making prevailing wage determinations and inspecting housing facilities for Mexican agricultural workers . . . are among the activities of the Farm Labor Service. The operation is carried out through the state employment security agencies and their local employment offices, each of which in agricultural areas has an indentifiable farm placement service with farm labor field representatives.

Job referrals for migratory labor are summarized:

	1957	1958
Number of crews	6,487	6,833
Number of individuals	145,736	162,610
Number of individuals over 16	120,548	134,362
Work schedules issued	6,758	7,492

Within this context two comments are revealing.

One appeared in the 1959 Texas Farm Placement report:

One fact stands out in an analysis of farm time and that is that the operation of the Mexican National program is not only time-consuming but that it is draining off too much of the available time. Time spent on the Mexican National program could be most profitably spent on the domestic farm program, but there is not sufficient time available for both. The Mexican National requirements are usually demand requirements; that is, an employer comes to the office in person for service. When this occurs the employer must be served before there is time available to get out of the office to do promotional and recruitment work. When enough of this type activity occurs, it can easily absorb all of the Farm time available in the office. In addition to the personal service requirements of the Mexican National program, there is also much time spent in preparation of authorizations, maintenance of order controls, maintenance of ceiling controls, wage surveys, and preparation of required reports. Actually, in a large number of offices, there is no time left in which to operate a domestic Farm Program after the demand requirements of the Mexican National program are met.

The second comment came from John Walsh, Executive Director of the President's Committee (November 18, 1960):

The farm labor problem is . . . part of a sickness in the agricultural industry. In too many instances growers have abdicated their management responsibility and surrendered their labor problem to a government agency.

Mr. Walsh added that the California Farm Bureau Federation had gone on record recognizing this fact by encouraging growers to recruit their own labor, provide training, plan for continuing employment, and provide wage differentials for jobs of varying complexity.

"Vertical Integration" in Agriculture

The information on the Di Giorgio Fruit Company comes from *Moody's Industrial Manual,* 1960 edition.

INDEX

domestic workers, 124, 130–31; tried in Washington, 124–25

Corporation farms: trend toward, 21; example of, 206–7

Country Life Commission: recommendations of (1910), 104

Connecticut: regulates intrastate transportation, 117

Crew leaders: federal registration proposed, 110; need for federal regulation of, 111, 119; and labor contractors, 118; exploitation of migrants by, 118–19, 225–26; and social security, 120; testimony of, 127–33; Florida class for, 154

Culture patterns: Mexican American migrants, 13–17, 135–39; Negro migrants, 25–28, 29–101, 169–72; common to many migrants, 38; Anglo migrants, 39–41; Navaho migrants, 41–43; Puerto Rican migrants, 43–45; braceros, 49–58; relation to health, 149–50

Delaware: first migrant child care center in, 177

Di Giorgio Fruit Company, 203–4; 206–7

Domestic migrants: defined, 23–24; difficulty of counting, 32; numbers and distribution by states, 33–34

Earnings: in Florida crops, 85–87; average annual, 123; in Texas, 123–24; regional comparisons, 124. *See also* Minimum wage

Education: federal legislation proposed, 110; special migrant schools, 159–62, 166; special problems of migrant children, 162–65; need for federal aid, 164–65; solutions, 165–66

Fair Labor Standards Act: excludes agriculture, 36, 210; farm labor coverage recommended, 104; child labor provision of, 122

Farm Bureau Federation, American: testimony of Matt Trigg, 64; stand on migrant education, 163; recommendations to state units, 211–12

Farm Bureau Federation, California:

stand on organized labor, 206; recommendation on recruitment, 237

Farmers. *See* Growers

Farm Placement Service: function of, 21, 235–36; migrant attitude toward, 21–22; annual worker plan of, 109; federal costs of, 235; demands of bracero program on, 236–37

Farm Security Administration: model farm labor camps, 105, 179

Farming. *See* Agriculture

Filipino labor: in California, 73

Florida: working conditions in, 85–87; 1957–58 emergency, 147–49; five-year health project, 154; migrant schools, 166; workshop for teachers, 166; bum blockades, 175

Foreign workers. *See* Braceros; Imported labor

Freeman, Orville, 210

Free wheelers: defined, 32; numbers undetermined, 34

Grange, California State: stand on organized labor, 206

Greene, Shirley, 68–69

Growers: organizations of, 60–1, 73, 196–97; attitudes toward labor, 68, 69, 208; increasing sensitivity of, 211; ethical concern of, 211; difficulties of small farmer, 233; abdication of management responsibility by, 237

Harrison, Burr F., 64–65

Harvesters: Migrant Ministry mobile units, 181–82

Hawaii: minimum wage in, 124; no residence laws in, 146; workmen's compensation compulsory in, 153

Hayes, Edward F., 203

Health of migrants: prevalent ills, 143; effects of mobility on, 144–46; attitudes toward illness, 150; insurance of, 152; Florida project, 154; California study, 227

Home base: defined, 20. *See also* Resettlement trend

Housing and sanitation: suggested codes, 106, 113; federal legislation proposed, 110; states with no regulations, 112; enforcement difficulties of, 113; growers' problems in, 113–14; regulation of in cities, 114; migrant attitudes toward, 114, 223; costs of, 223

Illinois: moves toward housing and sanitation regulation, 152–53

Imported labor: countries of origin, 32, 68, 74; numbers and distribution by states, 33–34; concentration in five states, 34. *See also* Braceros

Indian migrants: states and crops using, 41; culture patterns of, 41–43

Interstate Commerce Commission. *See* Transportation

Japanese migrants: Gentlemen's Agreement, 72

Labor: agriculture excluded from discussions of, 36. *See also* Organized labor

Labor contractors. *See* Crew leaders

Labor, Secretary of: conflict with Secretary of Agriculture, 64, 82, 222; controversial regulations issued by, 81. *See also* Mitchell, James P.

Labor, U. S. Department of, 202, 203

Latin: indentification preferred by Mexican Americans, 22

Legislation: proposed federal, 110; limitations of, 110

Lowry, Edith E., 184–45

Maryland: first migrant child care center in, 177

McGovern, George, 65

Mechanization: of beans, 128–29, 191–92; of tomatoes, 189–90; of cotton, 192–93; progress of, 192–94, 196; implications of, for migrants, 194–97, 212

Mexican American migrants: culture patterns of, 13–17, 23, 135–39; points of origin, 20; fear of authority, 22; persistence of folkways, 23; beginnings of immigration for farm work, 72–73; grower attitude toward, 74

Mexican nationals. *See* Braceros

Michigan: no housing or sanitation regulation in, 112; special migrant schools, 161; education project blocked in Berrien County, 163; mechanization of pickle harvest in, 193–94

Migrant farm workers: defined, 32; way of life, 35–37; characteristics of, 38, 143; motivations of, 38–39; projected need for, 194–96. *See also* Domestic migrants

Migrant Ministry: defined, 176; origin of, 176–77; demonstration role of, 177–78, 179, 180; role as referral agency, 180–81; state and local strength of, 182; consequences of social action by, 183–84. *See also* National Council of Churches

Miller, Max, 65

Minimum wage: federal legislation proposed, 110; none in 47 states, 124; existing federal legislation, 124; study of, in agriculture, 125, 226. *See also* Earnings

Minnesota: weakness of housing and sanitation code in, 113; tuberculosis crusade, 151–52; Roman Catholic school in, 161

Mississippi: cotton mechanization in, 193

Mitchell, James P., 82, 202, 203, 222. *See also* Labor, Secretary of

National Advisory Committee on Farm Labor, 62

National Child Labor Committee, 62, 161

National Conference on Labor Legislation (1945), 106

National Consumers League, 62, 161

National Council of Churches, 62, 184, 204. *See also* Migrant Ministry

National Council on Agricultural Life and Labor, 231

National Labor Relations Board: coverage of agriculture recommended, 104; no jurisdiction in agriculture, 210

Negro migrants: culture patterns of,

WASHINGTON COUNTY FREE LIBRARY
Hagerstown, Maryland
REgent 9-3250